Comments on other *Amazing Stories* from readers & reviewers

"Tightly written volumes filled with lots of wit and humour about famous and infamous Canadians."
Eric Shackleton, *The Globe and Mail*

"The heightened sense of drama and intrigue, combined with a good dose of human interest is what sets Amazing Stories *apart."*
Pamela Klaffke, *Calgary Herald*

"This is popular history as it should be... For this price, buy two and give one to a friend."
Terry Cook, a reader from Ottawa, on **Rebel Women**

"Glasner creates the moment of the explosion itself in graphic detail...she builds detail upon gruesome detail to create a convincingly authentic picture."
Peggy McKinnon, *The Sunday Herald,* on **The Halifax Explosion**

"It was wonderful...I found I could not put it down. I was sorry when it was completed."
Dorothy F. from Manitoba on **Marie-Anne Lagimodière**

"Stories are rich in description, and bristle with a clever, stylish realness."
Mark Weber, *Central Alberta Advisor,* on **Ghost Town Stories II**

"A compelling read. Bertin...has selected only the most intriguing tales, which she narrates with a wealth of detail."
Joyce Glasner, *New Brunswick Reader,* on **Strange Events**

"The resulting book is one readers will want to share with all the women in their lives"
Lynn Martel, *Rocky Mountain Outlook,* on **W**

FIGHTING FOR WOMEN'S RIGHTS

AMAZING STORIES®

FIGHTING FOR WOMEN'S RIGHTS

The Extraordinary Adventures
of Anna Leonowens

HISTORY/BIOGRAPHY

by Moushumi Chakrabarty

PUBLISHED BY ALTITUDE PUBLISHING CANADA LTD.
1500 Railway Avenue, Canmore, Alberta T1W 1P6
www.altitudepublishing.com
1-800-957-6888

Extreme care has been taken to ensure that all information presented in
this book is accurate and up to date. Neither the author nor the
publisher can be held responsible for any errors.

Publisher	Stephen Hutchings
Associate Publisher	Kara Turner
Editor	Dianne Smyth
Digital Photo Colouring	Bryan Pezzi

We acknowledge the financial support of the Government
of Canada through the Book Publishing Industry Development
Program (BPIDP) for our publishing activities.

Altitude GreenTree Program
Altitude Publishing will plant twice as many trees as were used
in the manufacturing of this product.

Library and Archives Canada Cataloguing in Publication Data

Chakrabarty, Moushumi
   Fighting for women's rights / Moushumi Chakrabarty.

(Amazing stories)
ISBN 1-55439-005-2

1. Leonowens, Anna Harriette, 1834-1914. 2. Governesses--Thailand--Biography.
3. Authors, English--19th century--Biography. 4. Feminists--Canada--Biography.
5. Suffragists--Canada--Biography.
I. Title. II. Series: Amazing stories (Canmore, Alta.)

PR4883.L64Z59 2005   823'.8   C2004-906268-9

Amazing Stories® is a registered trademark of Altitude Publishing Canada Ltd.

Printed and bound in Canada by Friesens
2 4 6 8 9 7 5 3 1

Ma and Baba — this, my first.

Anna Leonowens, Montreal, Quebec, 1910

Contents

Prologue

The trembling figure of the richly clad royal lady lay on the palace floor. Little Wanne, the princess, sobbed at the sight of her prostrate mother. She knew something terrible was about to happen.

Princess Wanne's mother, Lady Khoon Chom Kioa, had become so addicted to gambling that she had gambled away one of her daughter's servants. The little princess was so distraught that the king soon heard about the incident. He was furious and had summoned the lady to the audience hall to be sentenced for her offence, the violation of a taboo.

From his high golden throne, King Maha Mongkut of Siam uttered a harsh command. The entire court held its breath. Anna's eyes were wide with fear and she could feel Louis's fingers clutching at her skirts convulsively. Time hung suspended among the ornate chandeliers in the room. The cooling breeze that came in from the windows overlooking the bamboo groves suddenly stopped. Even the chattering monkeys swinging around the palace gardens seemed to have disappeared.

Suddenly, the huge wooden doors swung open, and two hefty women with evil-looking whips entered. Anna looked on in horror. The two chastisers bowed low to the king. Then, faces impassive, they advanced towards the terrified woman on the floor. The king abruptly nodded, his face black with fury. With a sudden jerk, the whips sang through the air. In a second, the floor beside the writhing woman turned red. Blood seeped through her blouse as it was torn open and the skin on her back parted. Lady Khoon Chom Kioa was left lying on the floor in agony.

And Anna was forever changed.

Chapter 1
Anna's Escape from Poverty and Servitude in India

Poona, a garrison town in 1849 British India, was like hundreds of other towns scattered throughout the country. Dusty narrow roads, old forts and palaces, green hamlets, and deep rivers all blended together to form a fascinating landscape. But there was hopelessness among the inhabitants, who were doomed by relentless poverty and stagnant opportunity.

In a cell-like barrack room, young Ann was unobtrusively trying to calculate how many days remained before her wedding day. Ann, who was normally quite composed, was nervous that morning. Her mother, noticing an unusual gleam in Ann's eyes, was looking at her suspiciously. The night before, Thomas "Leon" Owens, Ann's secret beau, had pulled her aside after church and asked her to be his wife. Now, in the heat of the morning, she was feeling slightly claustrophobic as she struggled to breathe in the crowded room where her mother was relentlessly snapping at Ann's younger siblings. She quickly turned away and faced the window while darning her brother's socks. The raucous sounds of the daily market soon dulled the squabbling inside the room. The fruit seller, who had just arrived, was standing directly below her window hawking his wares, and soldiers' wives were already haggling with the turbaned man. Noisy children skipped around him, touching the tempting mangoes, berries, and guavas, while the merchant made futile attempts to fend them off.

Heat rose in waves around the barracks and the sun glinted off the polished cannon, which stood in the middle of an enormous park. Far away on the hill Ann could see the brooding outline of the huge fort. Many years ago a princess had bravely fought to defend her territory from invaders, and the fort had become a symbol of strength and courage for Ann. She recalled the story, sung by the *sadhu* (holy man) when she was a child, about the princess who died fighting on a white horse on this very hill many hundreds of years ago. The story had greatly inspired her, and Ann silently vowed that she would rise above all this turmoil. Perhaps marriage to Leon was the first step.

Ann had no intention of being stuck in a barracks among squealing kids and quarrelling couples. But first, she would have to tell her mother and her stepfather that she intended to marry Leon, a clerk in the East India Company. She knew it would not be easy, which was why she had been seeing Leon secretly. Her stepfather had a violent temper and often took the strap to her younger brothers, who feared and hated him. Of course, she thought, he couldn't do anything to her. After all, she had already established her independent nature when she had insisted on going on a trip to the Middle East with the Reverend Badger. Ann knew that the others in the barracks gossiped mercilessly about her because she had travelled to foreign lands with a man who was not her husband. But Ann never did care what people thought of her. The trip had taken place just after her sister, Eliza, was married off to that insufferable sergeant major who was old enough to be a grandfather. Ann had been outraged. Another black mark against her stepfather, she thought with vehemence. He was the one who had arranged the marriage when her sister was only 15, a mere child. Ann began to think back to her sister's wedding day.

As she watched her older sister, Eliza, walking down the aisle, she had felt intensely anxious because she knew it was entirely possible that her stepfather was planning something similar for her. All around her she saw the heavily painted faces of the soldiers' wives who made up their social set. Most of the mean-tempered women from the barracks were heavy drinkers and sometimes their raucous laughter drove Ann mad. Scanning the faces of the assorted wedding guests and their rowdy children, she had hoped there was a way out, that she was not destined for such a life. In her young mind, Ann realized that she had no one to guide her, no one to suggest alternatives, no one to extend a helping hand. It was up to her alone to decide her fate. But she did have one friend she could talk to and that was the Reverend Badger, the chaplain of Poona's East India Company barracks. He had always been sympathetic towards her and he was aware of her dreams and her desire to learn more about the world. In fact, it was their discussions about her need to chart her own destiny that led to the infamous trip to Egypt.

Sitting in the pew, Ann looked at her mother, Mary Ann Glasscott, as if seeing her for the first time. This was the woman who had given birth to Ann and Eliza. Ann's brothers, who were quite a bit younger than she, had been born after her mother's second marriage. She wondered how her mother could ever have agreed to marry their stepfather. But Mary Ann Glasscott had not had much choice. She had been married to Infantryman Thomas Edwards, a cabinetmaker in service with the East India Company, and they had lived in the Poona army barracks. Life with her husband and their young daughter Eliza consisted of round after round of hard work and rationed food and drink. Then, when Mary Ann was three months pregnant with Ann, Thomas fell seriously ill and she had to care for him and Eliza, in addition to carrying out her assigned duties in the barracks. Three months before Ann's birth, Thomas died, leaving behind a pregnant widow and her young daughter. On November 5, 1831, Mary Ann's second baby girl, Ann Harriet Emma Edwards, was born into the most tenuous of circumstances. The other soldiers' wives felt pangs of sympathy for the young widow and mother but there was nothing they could do to help her. She would have to assess her limited options and learn to stand on her own two feet.

Unfortunately, army rules stated that a widow could stay on in the barracks for only a month or two after her husband died. Then the widow and her children would be turned out, alone and without support. Alternatively, the woman could marry another soldier and be allowed to stay. There were many men in the barracks who needed wives, but for every hundred men only six were allowed to have wives and families. So Mary Ann Glasscott had to marry the next available man in line or leave.

Ann knew in her heart that there was nothing else her mother could have done. She had been young and attractive but she had two very young children, no education, and little money. In those days, a sudden remarriage was considered quite an acceptable and practical solution. For Ann and Eliza's mother, it had been the only way out.

As Eliza's wedding ceremony proceeded, Ann began to think back on her childhood. She could not remember a single day when she did not desperately wish to be free from her situation. Sadly, although she had had Eliza for company, the sisters had absolutely nothing in common. Ann had lived in a world of her own making. She looked at Eliza and glumly reminisced about the days when they were both little girls. Ann had spent her early years holding on to her big sister's hand as they roamed the streets during their sparse playtime. Sometimes, if they were really lucky, they would come across the old sadhu telling ancient stories to the children under the old banyan tree. They attended the barracks school six days a week from the time they were four years old until the age of 15. A set of strict rules existed, particularly for the girls, who helped their mothers with meals, the laundry and mending, and the care of the younger children. When their education was deemed complete they were expected to marry or leave the barracks.

While they were still in school the children were taught English history, basic mathematics, and literature, but for most of the barracks children, school had no appeal whatsoever. Learning just added to the daily drudgery of their lives. Ann, on the other hand, was an avid learner who soaked up information and read anything and everything she could get her hands on. Study time was the most precious time of the day for her. She was a conscientious student who had found, in learning, an escape from the staleness of life around her. And this love of learning remained with her throughout her life. It was through books that Ann first developed an interest in the mythology of the East. The stories from the holy texts of India were rich in imagery, magic, and meaning, and she allowed herself to dream about them. Even in her final years of life, she derived much pleasure and comfort from reading and contemplating the holy books of the Hindus.

Eliza was an entirely different person. She was glad when she was finished with school even though few opportunities existed for her and the other "army rats." Most girls from the barracks became wives of men similar to their fathers. A lucky few became nurses or teachers, but this was rare, and Eliza had no such ambitions. When her last school term ended, she obediently fell in with the marriage plans their stepfather concocted. Ann, who fully intended to escape the same fate, was disgusted with the 38-year-old man about to become her brother-in-law. All she could see in him were his large sweaty hands and his loose mouth.

A short time after Eliza's wedding, Ann spoke to Reverend Badger about her fear that she might also become the victim of her stepfather's eager plotting. The reverend knew that opportunities were very limited for someone of Ann's gender, no matter how intelligent she was. Coincidentally, at the time of this conversation, he was in the midst of making plans to depart on a long trip to the Middle East. The ancient countries he spoke of made Ann's breath come faster — Egypt, Babylon, Mesopotamia — the wondrous lands of pharaohs and fabled gardens. Reverend Badger asked her if she would consider accompanying him as a scribe. Ann was enthralled with these exotic places so it was an easy decision for her. Knowing of her interest in history, cultures, and languages, the reverend had thought about approaching her to join him on the journey long before Anna had expressed her discontent and her fears. But he hadn't asked her before Eliza's wedding because he was afraid his offer might be misconstrued. Ann could hardly believe her ears. She was so keen to go that she completely dismissed the possibility that people would look down on her, and she chose not to listen to the gossipmongers' hurtful innuendoes that followed. It was of no consequence, people would always talk, she told her mother (who secretly supported her dreams all along). But there was something that Ann did not tell her mother before the trip, and that was that she and Leon Owens were becoming serious about one another.

Leon had been completely open with Ann, telling her that, because of his straitened circumstances, he could not possibly commit to an engagement until circumstances changed for him. This had put Ann in a very vulnerable position because she had just completed her own schooling. She knew that her stepfather was already thinking about marrying her off and would soon be negotiating with his barracks buddies. Ann was well aware of the army decree, and she knew that she would soon be faced with a choice — either get married or leave the barracks. If she married she would be caught up in the same hopeless cycle that her mother and sister had fallen into.

So, despite considerable family opposition and obvious social disapproval, Ann took the bold step of leaving the barracks to board a ship bound for the Middle East with an unmarried man. (There is speculation among scholars about this trip. Some historians say Reverend Badger's wife accompanied them on the tour; others claim that there is no record of his having been married at all.) When all the arrangements were finalized, the Reverend Badger and Ann sailed away from the neighbouring port of Bombay. As the ship left the harbour, Ann stood on the deck and looked back at the land with a sense of triumph. She had made it this far without giving in. Despite her mother's hand-wringing and tears and her stepfather's thundering and swearing, Ann had embarked on a journey that, in her young life, was a major event in more ways than one. Her family and neighbours must have been amazed, not only by her audacity, but also at the extent of her confidence and determination in the face of so much opposition.

Familiar land quickly slipped away, and they were soon deep into the lanes of the Arabian Sea. The exhilarating sea air helped Ann leave the gossip and whispers behind. The trip was an incredible experience and, while travelling through the markets of Egypt and visiting the desert landscapes, Ann made copious notes for the reverend and for herself. Everything was new and fascinating to her. The veiled women of Egypt, the enormous pyramids, and the camel rides through the desert profoundly impressed her. She remained steadfast that she had done the right thing by going on this adventurous journey, and she knew, intuitively, that this first adventure would alter her destiny. And it certainly did. After touring many fabulous countries, Ann boarded a ship for the return to India and went back to her family. But deep inside her were an insatiable wanderlust and a growing core of inner strength. Nothing had changed in Poona — except Ann. A sense of individuality and independence had taken root, and it continued to flower throughout her life.

At that time, Poona was famous for its bands of armed men, caparisoned elephants, gorgeous palanquins (covered one-person litters), and bejewelled horses, which paraded on the streets as rich governors and potentates of British and Indian heritage flaunted their wealth. Outdoor weddings and numerous celebrations were commonplace because of Poona's bracing climate. In contrast, Bombay, which was just next door, was hot and muggy and not nearly so lively. Poona, with its two rivers, its distant vista of blue mountains, and its scores of pipal trees, was considered a paradise. Not so for the barracks personnel, however. Now even more conscious of the disparity between social classes, Ann noted that even the barracks boys, children as young as six, were forced to work long hours alongside their fathers. And women like her mother still took in the laundry and repaired the uniforms of the military men in order to make enough extra money to survive. They worked non-stop from the time they awoke in the early morning until they fell into bed, exhausted, late at night.

After her return Ann grew increasingly restless, until she met up with Leon again. They soon made up their minds to strike out together and they became engaged. Ann decided the time was now or never, so one day, while her mother was catching her breath with a cup of tea, Ann broke the news to her. Mary Ann could hardly believe Ann's announcement. Engaged to be married! Mary Ann had not even known about the relationship. And Leon was only a clerk, not a soldier. Ann's mother was greatly alarmed, as she knew how her husband would react. He would be absolutely furious. Mary Ann was conscious that Ann had matured considerably since her trip abroad, and had become more determined than ever. But she had always known that Ann was different from the rest of her children. For one thing, her love of reading and writing had set her apart, and it was because of this marked difference that Ann was clearly resented by others in the family and in the entire community. However, the girl was now of age, and Mary Ann knew there was nothing on earth that could prevent her from making her own decision.

As expected, Ann's stepfather was enraged upon hearing the news. He claimed that his main objection was that he had not known about this developing affair. And to top it off, the lad wasn't even a military man! However, he finally calmed down when he realized that there was no way he could prevent Ann from marrying Leon. So, later that year, after considerable ridicule and criticism, Ann and Leon were married. During the small gathering at the Poona cantonment church Ann looked radiant, as all new brides do, but her elation may have also been because she was about to escape the narrow strictures of life in the barracks.

The couple immediately left for Bombay to set up their home. Ann knew Leon well and was aware of her considerable influence over him. As the stronger of the two, Ann made all the decisions. Leon was too much in awe of his educated and well-travelled bride to make many suggestions regarding their future. Leon knew that Ann would not be content to stay in one place. Ann effortlessly convinced Leon that moving from place to place would broaden their outlook as well as their prospects. And once Ann made up her mind about something, nothing could stop her.

Eventually, Anne bore two children who did not survive. She hovered anxiously over her first baby while it was sickening but the *dai* (midwife), who had helped her with the birth, sadly shook her head at the gasping baby. After the burial of her first child, Ann resolved to be strong and not give way to weakness or emotion. Soon after, Ann was pregnant again, but her second baby was stillborn. By this time the young couple were so devastated that they found it a strain to be civil to the mourners who called.

Ann desperately wished to have another child and, in time, she did bear two children who survived: a daughter, Avis Connybeare, followed by a son, Louis Thomas Gunnis. Giving birth in British India was one thing, but rearing children and keeping them safe from cholera, whooping cough, and mosquito bites in the villages and towns was another.

Nevertheless, Leon, Ann, and their young family travelled across British India in a restless search for work for Leon. Although life was challenging, it was an adventure to Ann. She constantly added to her knowledge base while making her home in different places across a vast land of myriad influences and customs. It was not easy going from one place to another; living hand to mouth while Leon found work in temporary situations. The family travelled by boat, bullock cart, and train across heavily forested land where the threat of *thugees* loomed large. These groups of bloodthirsty armed bandits were legendary for sparing no one, not even women and children, and Ann spent many sleepless nights en route. She would lie awake guarding her small children in the various places where they put up for the night. Wild animals were also a real danger. And high in the hills of some provinces, the stories of man-eating tigers dragging away infants were enough to drive anyone crazy with fear.

It was during this sojourn that Ann received the news that her mother had died. For Ann, it was as if the bond with her family had suddenly snapped. After her marriage she had rarely visited her siblings, and her relationship with her stepfather had remained acrimonious. Her mother's passing seemed to bring closure to her old life and, although Ann mourned, she found the strength to move away from her family without looking back.

Eventually, Leon was offered a job in Singapore as the manager of a small hotel. For Ann it meant a chance to travel to a new place, so there was no hesitation on her part. She was eager to start a new life in Singapore. Besides, in India, slowly but surely, things were changing. There was talk about a rebellion, and rumours were rife about a plot to overthrow the British. No longer could the British be certain that their native servants and *sepoys* (native Indian soldiers under British discipline) would support them against their own people. So the young Owens family left India with a sense of relief and moved to a new home in exotic southeast Asia. Ann could not help rejoicing in her good fortune, as her children's health improved dramatically and they were all enthralled with their new environment. Though they were not very well off, Ann was truly happy for the first time in her life.

In 1857, the political rumours became a reality and an event took place in British India, the echoes and tremors of which were felt even in faraway London. The Sepoy Mutiny shook the very foundations of British rule in India. Thousands of women and children from both the British and the Indian sides were massacred. A mob of Indian soldiers marched to Delhi, where they proclaimed an ailing Moghul emperor, Bahadur Shah Zafar, as their sovereign. The whole country was suddenly in turmoil. But Ann, safe and content in her new home, was far from the madness that was engulfing India.

Two years later, in 1858, tragedy struck. Leon died suddenly from an unknown cause, and Ann was instantly thrust into a position similar to that of her mother before her. She had become a widow at a very young age with two children to rear. However, Ann was more determined than ever to avoid the kind of life her mother and sister had fallen into. First, she decided that she would not remarry. Second, she decided that she must, at all costs, avoid any situation that offered little chance for improvement. She wanted something better for her children, but she had very little money, no fat pension, no family to help her out, and almost no connections. How was an impoverished widow to survive when faced with being the sole provider for her family?

In those days, the Victorians admired the idea of a brave ,lone woman having to earn her living through honourable means. But Ann realized that without an acceptable past, it would be nearly impossible to sustain her family without a man in her life. If, on the other hand, she were from a "good family," she would be applauded and encouraged for her bravery and her piety. But what could she possibly do to create a prestigious background?

Without wasting any time at all, Ann decided to change her identity. She invented a new persona and began to call herself Anna Leonowens. Overnight, she miraculously became the widow of a high-ranking military officer, forced through circumstance to earn her living. She fabricated a respectable background, figuring it would go down well with the class-conscious British establishment — and she permanently severed all ties with her family back in India. These were the first steps in her remarkable transformation from

Ann Harriet Emma Owens to Anna Leonowens.

From that time on, whenever she was asked about her background, Anna claimed that she had been born into an old Welsh family in Carnevon. She gave her year of birth as 1834, three years after her actual birth. Anna told people that her father had died, and that when her mother remarried her stepfather had taken custody of the family homestead in Wales. Then, she claimed that, against her stepfather's wishes, she had married a dashing military officer, Thomas Leonowens, for which her stepfather disinherited her, and that this act had rendered her penniless. To top off her story, Anna claimed that her husband died in her arms after suffering a heat stroke in the aftermath of a tiger hunt in Singapore. By this time, her listeners were usually dabbing their eyes in sympathy for the brave young Mrs. Leonowens.

For the next few years, Anna travelled to various garrison towns in southeast Asia teaching English literature, basic mathematics, and history to the children of British officers stationed in the Orient. No one would have sent their children to her if they had suspected her origins. Exotic places such as Sarawak, Borneo, and Singapore became temporary homes to Anna, Avis, and Louis. As they sailed up mysterious rivers to strange towns, Anna became more and more convinced that her decision to leave her life in India behind was the right one. Though her new life was apt to be anything but steady, it offered them novel experiences and the chance of something big just around the corner. Anna had always relished the new and the out of the ordinary. The countries of southeast Asia presented her with an ever-changing platter of delights. In addition, her love for the languages and customs of the Orient flourished and remained with her for the rest of her life.

Anna never let her guard down, not even for a moment. When there were whispers about her background, she maintained an enigmatic silence. (It was only through later research, many years after her death in Montreal, that details of her early life began to emerge. An eminent scholar, Dr. W.S. Bristowe, searching through records in Wales, stumbled upon the truth — that Anna had been born in India in very humble circumstances.) Remarkably, just four years after the death of her husband, Anna was a completely transformed woman, a single parent, and an educator. The metamorphosis was now complete. Anna resolutely turned her back on her past and moved forward with her children, determined to give them a life free of poverty and stigma.

Chapter 2
Life in the Royal Court of Siam

Anna's long strides through the narrow streets of Singapore's Chinatown took her past the teahouse where regulars were sitting outside enjoying the morning sun. The temple spire glinted and small songbirds in cages fluttered their wings. Even though she was a little late, her mind was teeming with questions as she wondered why William Adamson, branch manager of the Borneo Company, had asked to see her. Anna pulled her gold watch out from her blouse and checked the time, then made a quick decision. She would simply have to hail a rickshaw.

As she climbed in, she resumed her thoughts. William Adamson's two children were Anna's students. She hoped they were not being withdrawn from her school because she was already having difficulty making ends meet. Her own children, Avis and Louis, were just learning to cope with life after their father's death. The rent for their two-room flat was all she could afford and she needed more students, not fewer. (There is some doubt among historians as to whether or not Anna actually ran a school. Some propose that she may have been a teaching assistant-headmistress somewhere. No matter. It was a difficult time for Anna.) As they wove through the streets at a frantic pace, the rickshaw puller shook his head, calling out in shrill tones to passersby and ringing a metal bell to alert pedestrians. Anna told him to stop directly in front of the tall buildings of the Borneo Company, where she alighted and paid the man. With her parasol in one hand, Anna picked up her skirts and climbed the wide marble steps nodding to the uniformed doorman, who saluted her smartly when she reached the top step.

Adamson welcomed her warmly and offered her a seat. Anna looked inquiringly at him. Although she appeared calm, no one could have guessed how fast her heart was beating. What he said next so astonished her that she was at a loss for words. He asked her if she would be interested in accepting a position as governess at the royal court in Siam (renamed Thailand in 1939). The king of Siam needed a governess who would tutor his children and wives in English. Adamson explained that when Tan Kim Ching, the king's consul in Singapore, had told him that the royal palace at Bangkok needed a reliable governess, Anna immediately came to his mind. Adamson had told the consul that he could personally endorse Mrs. Leonowens's reputation as a good teacher.

Tan Kim Ching had stressed that the king needed someone who, in addition to being an excellent teacher, would be sensitive to the protocol that the position demanded. The king's consul was emphatic that teachers with missionary zeal were not acceptable. Adamson assured the consul by telling him about Anna's talent as a storyteller and added that his own children were always singing her praises. In addition, he emphasized that her stories were interesting and wholesome moralistic statements, without religious overtones.

Adamson told Anna to expect a letter from the king of Siam offering her the position of governess for the enormous sum of £100 per month in addition to lodging and meals in the palace grounds. Adamson explained that the king's intention was that his wives and children increase their knowledge of the English language and learn about science and literature. Masking her growing excitement, Anna promised to give the matter serious thought. She agreed to let him know in two days if she would accept the offer, although in her mind and heart Anna had already made her decision. As she walked home, her mind raced, calculating the pros and cons of the amazing offer. There was no doubt it would be a great boost for her financially. It would also give her a chance to become acquainted with a better class of people, and Avis and Louis would greatly benefit from this. Anna felt sure they would jump at the chance to live in a royal household.

That afternoon, with a still-flushed face, Anna gave her students a lesson about the hand of destiny leading those who believe. Later, as she had predicted, her own two children were extremely excited by the news. Louis especially was fired up with the thought that he would see a real king. Avis, the quieter of the two, simply smiled contentedly when her mother told her that their money troubles were over.

Anna was astounded, however, at the reaction of her friends and acquaintances, who were horrified that she was even considering such an offer. They pointed out, delicately at first, that there were dangers in a country like Siam. She would have to deal with all manner of people. They warned her she would have to step carefully in case she committed some faux pas that would offend royal sensibilities. And, they pointed out, Siam was not England. Anna was a widow with two young children, for whose moral upbringing she was responsible. Who knew what went on in the harems of Siam? What about the pagan influence on the children's characters?

In February of 1862, Anna received the king of Siam's letter offering her employment in the royal household and emphasizing that discussion of any kind regarding Christianity would not be tolerated. Anna considered her position carefully. She knew her friends had her best interests at heart, but she was accustomed to making her own decisions. For a very long time now, she had trusted her instincts. She looked around the tiny room where she and Avis had a little bed. The mirror above the washstand was cracked and the wallpaper was peeling. Though the room was neat, it reflected a distressing hopelessness. She then tiptoed to the next room, where five-year-old Louis was sleeping, limbs askew. Anna felt a sharp pang of maternal love. She simply had to give her children a better life than one of genteel poverty.

Anna's mind was made up, but there was one complication — Avis. If the environment in Siam proved to be inappropriate (such as being fertile ground for the corruption of a young girl's mind and morals), it might affect her future opportunities. Reluctantly, Anna decided that she would have to send Avis, who was now eight years old, to boarding school in London, England. After all, it was a common practice in those days for families who lived in the Orient. Her heart was torn as she looked at the young innocent face on the pillow next to her. How would she live without this dear, calm influence in her life? Tears welled up in her eyes, but Anna knew she had to be strong. She broke the news to the children the next day.

Watching the ship sail away with Avis was one of the hardest things Anna did in her entire life. As she waved her white kerchief, she felt as though her heart would break. A sob escaped her, and Louis, who was crying openly, grasped his mother's hand tightly. Then mother and son went back to their empty quarters and wept for their loved one, who was now alone on a ship. The hardest thing for both of them was knowing that they would have to wait for months to hear that Avis had safely reached her destination.

The next morning, with an extremely heavy heart, Anna began the process of settling her affairs in Singapore in preparation for her journey to Siam. One of the first things she did was hire a tutor, Munshi, to accompany her and Louis to Siam. Munshi's wife, Bibi, would act as housekeeper. Anna then bid goodbye to the children who had studied under her guidance at the tiny school and began to think about the new students she would soon be teaching. When her friends and acquaintances found that she could not be dissuaded from her venture, they either cut her off completely or warmly applauded her courage and strength.

Thus, in 1862, Anna sailed up the Chao Phya Menam River into the fabled kingdom of Siam to accept her new position as governess at the court of King Maha Mongkut. From the deck on the steamer, Anna gazed in amazement at the scene around her. The low banks of the river teemed with life. An abundance of fruit trees as well as cocoa and areca palms decorated the fertile land of Siam. She marvelled at the wooden houses, the gilded spires of temples and pagodas, and the rice fields that stretched out toward the distant limestone hills. White-sailed boats slowly navigated the broad muddy river, churning up the innards of the waterway. Anna and Louis looked on in fascination, absorbing a multitude of sights and sounds: the flash of boldly darting kingfishers, the swarthy brown backs of labourers with sacks of produce, and the running creeks and canals beside the stone ruins of temples. Yellow-robed monks wound their way through the lanes.

Anna spotted a white chapel with green windows. A sign indicated it was the American Presbyterian Mission, and she immediately recalled William Adamson's warning that religious references were to be strictly avoided. The king of Siam was concerned about the possibility of his subjects converting to Christianity. His relationship with the missionaries was cordial — as long as they kept their distance and did not interfere in his affairs. Anna, more than a little nervous about meeting the reputedly temperamental monarch, was at the same time impressed by King Mongkut's immense knowledge and his awareness of world religions and of spirituality. She knew he had ascended the throne of Siam late in life and that he had spent most of his adult years as a Buddhist monk, with little interest in acquiring a kingdom. Perhaps he wouldn't be so formidable after all.

As they approached the harbour landing, it appeared that there was no one from the palace waiting on shore to receive her. Suddenly, Louis shouted and pointed to a long gondola-like boat that looked somewhat like a dragon. It was coming towards them, slicing swiftly through the river. The boat suddenly stopped beside them. A regal man dressed in a purple loincloth, with his torso bare, calmly stepped into the boat — and all of those assembled, except Anna and Louis, prostrated. Through an interpreter, he introduced himself as the prime minister. Anna curtsied and told Louis to bow. Within minutes the royal entourage got back into their boat and sailed away.

After the royal boat left, Anna realized that there had been no mention of accommodation. She felt a moment of pure panic. Where would she take Louis, Munshi, and Bibi when the steamer docked? Where would they sleep that night? It was already dusk, and people were leaving the docks. The air was alive with the sounds of birds roosting, and little fires were springing up across the landscape. Anna turned to the captain, who happened to be standing beside her. He seemed a little embarrassed when she mentioned her predicament but, in the end, arranged a makeshift bed on the steamer. Anna settled down beside Louis for the night, though sleep did not come easily. What had she let herself in for? During the night, fears and insecurities filled her mind, and the ache for her far away daughter increased tenfold. Now in a strange land, where she knew no one, she was truly worried about the future and began to wonder what kind of a situation she would be faced with in the morning.

However, Anna was ever the optimist. Things always look better in the morning, she thought. Besides, the prime minister himself had come to see her. Surely the palace would arrange something the next day. As Anna finally drifted off to sleep, she was soothed by the steamer gently rocking as waves lapped at its sides. Only the sound of Munshi's snoring on the mat outside her cabin broke the silence on the water.

Anna and her three dependants left the steamer in the morning rested and ready to face a new day. Armed with confidence in her ability to get things done, Anna soon found lodgings for the four of them and arranged for the delivery of their belongings to their quarters. Louis was beside himself with excitement at the strange activities around him. The bald monks begging for alms, the mounds of exotic fruits on the roadside stalls, a cow snorting in anger at a rickshaw puller, mynah birds mocking each other from the trees — all these things fascinated him as he waited beside his mother in the street. Their new home was not at all what Anna had imagined it would be, and the noise in the street was enough to make a person deaf. Obviously, privacy was going to be an issue, she thought, as hordes of curious neighbours descended on them, crowding around the doorway. Giggling excited children pushed their way into the rooms, and then raced back to their mothers to report what they had seen inside. Bibi had a hard time shooing out the friendly intruders, and Anna, her trembling legs having given way, collapsed into a corner. Finally, a soldier arrived carrying a summons. Anna was to meet with the king the very next morning. She prayed for patience and hoped that the audience would go well.

The next morning, in the great palace hall, King Mongkut arrived in a towering rage. Something serious must have happened to bring this on, thought Anna. Though he was revered as a just ruler who had implemented progressive reforms in Siamese society, Anna found herself having mixed feelings and hoped she would be able to stand up to this exhibition of temper. So, with Louis beside her, she stood in trepidation waiting her turn to speak at the great palace hall.

After a long wait, the king welcomed her in a very formal manner and explained that his children and wives would be her students. They were all keen to learn English. She was to be paid the previously agreed salary and would be given a house inside the royal compound. He said nothing beyond that, so Anna decided to let him know how she felt. She cleared her throat and pointed out that she would much prefer a house outside the palace, making it clear to the king that she was not at all satisfied with her present living arrangement. The king was shocked by her assertive manner. All around him were prostrated courtiers — and there was complete silence in the richly decorated hall. Anna politely restated that her living quarters were unsuitable and that she needed something better for her young son. Rapid questions followed. How old was Anna? Why was her husband not with her? How was she managing without a male figure?

A westerner would have considered the king's barrage of questions to be inappropriate, personal, and very rude. But Anna was worldly enough to know that each culture has its own code of behaviour. When she had satisfied the king's curiosity about her circumstances, Anna was told that her request for a house outside the palace would be looked into at a later date. Further, if she changed her mind about living inside the palace grounds, she was to let the prime minister know. Anna was then introduced to her pupils as they lined up in front of her. The king obviously had a great love for his children and called out each by name. They folded their palms together and bowed their heads to show respect to their new governess. Anna was instantly charmed by their demeanour. After meeting her charges, she took leave of the king, and was taken to the enclosed pavilion where she would soon be teaching English to the royal children and a number of the king's wives. Lessons would begin the next day.

Anna became engaged with the task at hand. She was a patient but demanding teacher who quickly earned the respect of her students. But, as always in her life, she took great care to listen to and learn from her students. She spent a lot of her time in the royal court in conversation with the women, learning about their lives in the harem, their loneliness, their insecurities, and their modest joys. Anna spent a great deal of time after classes thinking about the lives of these women and trying to understand their culture.

After six months, Anna finally heard from Avis. Upon reading that her young daughter had reached England safely and was adjusting to her new life in an English boarding school, Anna heaved a sigh of relief. From that moment on she was able to immerse herself in her work and to fully appreciate life in Siam. In the months that followed, Anna took great pleasure in riding around the streets of Bangkok in a rickshaw in her constant quest to acculturate herself. On these outings she visited the most prominent of the many monasteries. Buddhism, overlaid with ancient Hindu customs and rituals, was the dominant religion in Siam, and monasteries occupied a very important place in the social and political fabric of the country. Anna learned about the significant passages in the Buddha's life, and studied the prayers and thanksgiving psalms addressed to the Perfect One. She visited the monasteries' libraries, which were full of manuscripts written on palm leaves and ivory tablets. The Buddhist moral code, which was inscribed on these materials in ornate gold lettering, was endlessly fascinating to her.

The Siamese loved their native poetry, music, lyrics, ballads, and theatre, and Anna began to realize that drama played an important role in their lives and culture. Along with Louis, she attended many cultural events in the palace compound. The Hindu epics, the *Ramayana* and the *Mahabharata* were very popular. "Now watch, my dear, how Krishna comes to the rescue of Draupadi, the proud princess, when she is being shamed in the court," she would whisper to a spellbound Louis. The epics had a deep meaning for Anna, as she already knew most of these stories by heart, having heard them many times in her childhood in India.

The only citizens allowed to attend the palace performances were the royal ladies and their children. There was always an air of merriment when news of a performance filtered through the various strands of court gossip. Louis would greet the news with a whoop of excitement and with his dear friend, Prince Chulalongkorn, would beg Anna to attend, too. Anna was conscious that theatre was the only entertainment in the very controlled lives of the harem women, who were subject to strict palace rules about behaviour and deportment. These enduring women often waited for months before being summoned to see the king.

The school where Anna taught was inside the palace courtyard, in a pavilion where men were not permitted to enter. She taught the little ones the English alphabet and the nursery rhymes so beloved by scores of children everywhere. In their sarongs and tiny blouses, their long straight hair adorned with fresh jasmine, the youngest of Anna's pupils soon endeared themselves to her. They were all a little intimidated by the stern-faced woman, who looked so different from them. If she did not like what she saw, she made sure the children understood the reason for her displeasure. But despite her strict demeanour, she was genuinely fond of her charges. And they loved her fantastic stories.

The older children and the ladies of the royal court learned the alphabet, reading, writing, and arithmetic. In the balmy morning sunshine of Siam, they would recite the English alphabet, sing English rhymes, and ponder the fascinating tales that Anna told them. Her storytelling skills were finely honed during this time, as was her growing awareness of the role of women across cultures. Anna was always as eager to learn as she was to teach and she quickly discovered that she could not remain aloof from goings on in the palace.

One of these involved the punishment of a royal lady who had gambled away one of her daughter's servants. Lady Khoon Chom Kioa, one of the king's wives, had a young daughter, Princess Wanne. Since most of the harem ladies passed a good deal of their time lounging, they were sometimes drawn to idle or forbidden pursuits. This particular wife had fallen victim to the lure of gambling — a taboo in Siamese culture — and had gambled away one of her daughter's servants. For this, she was sentenced to a whipping. Anna was mortified at the barbarity of what she witnessed and later wrote in her first book (1870), "It was horrible to witness such an abuse of power." Anna's guilt about not speaking out in the woman's defence stayed with her day and night.

Another incident involving one of the harem ladies brought the full extent of the king's wrath on Anna's head. Lady Son Klin (Hidden Perfume) was a Siamese lady of noble birth, who had been out of favour with the king for many years. She was, however, one of Anna's favourite students, and they eventually became good friends. Hidden Perfume was diligent, painstaking, and always eager to learn. Perhaps influenced by Anna's bold and confident manner, she sent her son, Prince Krita, who was the centre of her universe, to the king with a petition regarding one of her relatives. Things went awry, however, and the infuriated king accused Hidden Perfume of being a spy, a traitor, and a liar — and sentenced her to the dungeons. Right before Anna's eyes, Hidden Perfume was beaten with a slipper, the humiliating social sanction meted out to liars throughout Siam. Her anguished sobs echoed through the palace as she was dragged away to the dungeons. It was more than Anna could bear. This time she had to speak out. What became Anna's lifelong compassion for women and her sense of social justice began with these two incidents. Many years later, when describing her feelings about some of the traumatic incidents she had witnessed or heard about, she recalled:

> *How I pitied those ill-fated sisters of mine, imprisoned without a crime! If they could have but rejoiced once more in the freedom of the fields and woods, what new births of gladness might have been theirs — they who with a gasp of despair and moral death first entered those royal dungeons, never again to come forth alive!*
>
> (Leonowens, 1870, *The English Governess at the Siamese Court*)

A short time after the sentencing of Hidden Perfume, knowing that she had an elevated status in the eyes of the king, Anna decided she would do all she could to help this unfortunate lady of the court. Anna and the king had often talked at length about matters involving the moral and spiritual laws that govern humanity. So, after King Mongkut had calmed down, she appealed to him to think about justice and to set matters right. At first the king was astounded that she had the temerity to question his judgment in matters that did not concern her. But she pointed out that it was wrong to imprison people when the only evidence against them was half-formed supposition and gossip. She reminded him that Hidden Perfume had a young son who was desperately unhappy without his mother. Surely the king, being a kind and fair ruler, could see that the sentence was unjust? The king was furious.

Their conversations on this matter went on for days, most ending in the same way. She would regroup and come back again when she sensed the king would listen. Finally, after many discussions, Anna pointed out that Hidden Perfume was her pupil, and thus her responsibility. This time the king was silent when she left. Her words finally seemed to be having some effect, and the by-now-troubled king said he would think further about the situation.

When Anna returned to teach school the following day, she learned with immense relief that Hidden Perfume had been set free and reunited with her son, Prince Krita. Anna later wrote that Hidden Perfume never forgot her intervention, and as a token of her regard, gave Anna an emerald ring that she wore to the end of her days in faraway Canada.

Once Hidden Perfume's story became known, Anna found herself inundated with appeals and the petitioners lined up in front of her door every morning. As she swiftly completed her toilette and ate a breakfast of fresh mango, papaya, and tea, the murmurs of the supplicants standing patiently as the sun rose in the sky, mingled with the sounds of Chinese coolies squabbling, the shriek of parrots, and the rattling of the monks' bowls as they made their rounds to collect alms. It was a nuisance, she thought, but what could she do? She could not turn away these poor people who had taken it into their heads that this *farang* (foreigner) had the ear of the king himself. Her sense of justice could not tolerate the monarch's dictatorial ways and, gradually, she found herself sympathizing with the common people's quarrels over land and money and their petitions for special favours from the king.

Though she was content with her position in Siam, one thing continued to rankle. The king had still not made adequate arrangements for her to move to a more suitable house in Bangkok, and Anna continued to refuse accommodation in the palace compound. And the king, who was just as stubborn as Anna, did nothing about it. The situation eventually became problematic because, increasingly, she found herself helping the king with his correspondence and reports. He had many dealings with Europeans and he often asked Anna to help with the copying, correcting, dictating, reading, and translating. Anna soon found that she was often working until 10 o'clock at night. These long hours seemed to have become an expected part of her job in the palace, but the extra work was not a part of her employment agreement. The strain eventually began to affect her health and, by the summer of 1886, after nearly six years in Siam, Anna's health had noticeably deteriorated. The English doctor attending her shook his head and told her what she had already guessed

— she was overworked and needed a lengthy rest. The heat was also a problem. With her voluminous skirts and lace-up boots, Anna never had a chance to cool off. Early mornings were tolerable and so were late evenings, but the days passed in a kind of fever, even though she shaded her head with a parasol on her way to the palace. It was not enough that the palace courtyard had fountains and curtains of woven grasses. She craved cooler climates and fantasized about snow and ice.

Something else was also gnawing at Anna — her desperate longing to see Avis. She was frequently anxious and beset with fears about her daughter. Suppose she, Anna, were to die? What would happen to Avis and Louis? With these fears weighing heavily on her mind, she decided to apply to the king for leave. Anna was determined to take a lengthy holiday in England.

Predictably, King Mongkut was upset at the prospect of losing Anna. He stormed about saying that finding a reliable replacement for her would be quite difficult. He fumed that there was much work to be done. But Anna remained firm in her demand. After much deliberation, the king finally granted her a six-month leave of absence. Louis was almost 11 years old at the time and had grown perhaps too fond of his carefree palace life in Siam. Anna did not want him to get ideas that would prove above his station in the real world. Her husband's relatives, with whom she had stayed in contact, had suggested a school in Dublin, Ireland, that would instil the values that Anna wanted in her son. Louis was distraught at the idea of going away. He was not interested in a conventional education and he loathed Latin, mathematics, and the classics. He was a free spirit who was in his element while hunting, shooting, and riding. In addition, he had developed a strong bond with Prince Chulalongkorn, who was later to succeed his father as king. Louis clearly did not want to leave, particularly to live in a boarding school in cold far-away Ireland.

By July of 1867, Anna had finalized her arrangements to leave Bangkok. She stood at her bedroom window at dawn on the morning of her departure, watching the flock of parakeets that launched from the nearby tree. Her years in Siam had been good ones, and she had developed and nurtured close friendships. But above all she had discovered what it meant to stand up for one's rights, to depend on oneself, and to take the responsibility that came with being a single parent in a foreign country. Anna felt an unexpected sadness for her pupils, some of whom, with tears in their eyes, had begged her to stay. Her favourite student, Prince Chulalongkorn, was also upset that "Anna mem" and his good friend Louis were leaving. Anna had managed to instil in the prince values and ideas like her own. He did not like the way slaves were treated and was often shocked and frustrated by the way the royal household dealt with them. The prince had been significantly influenced by Anna's teachings.

At the quay, where the ship that would take Anna and

Louis away stood waiting, there was a commotion when the king arrived unannounced to say goodbye to his governess. He made a speech in honour of Anna, saying that, although he found her a "difficult woman," she was "a good and true lady." The king then presented Louis with a generous gift of £100. After the king left, other people also pressed gifts on Anna and Louis. Fresh fruit and vegetables, bolts of cloth, and even a squawking chicken were among the bounty. All of Bangkok seemed to have a soft spot for the fiery farang who was leaving them. Prince Chulalongkorn arrived last in his palanquin to bid goodbye to his teacher and friend. As he shook hands with her, requesting that she return to Bangkok after her holiday, she was moved to tears by his poignant farewell.

Louis watched with tears in his eyes as the shoreline of Siam receded into the distance. As Anna stood on the deck, lost in her thoughts, the Reclining Buddha passed before her eyes. It was a huge 100-metre long figure that resided at the Wat Po complex. As long as she lived Anna never forgot what an old monk had explained to her during a visit to that monastery — that Buddhism teaches spiritual matters and a belief in social equality — a philosophy that was in accordance with her own beliefs. The teachings of the Buddha, the simplicity of the Siamese people, and the love they had bestowed on Anna would prove unforgettable. As she embarked on her long journey to England, Anna began to realize that she was destined to spend the rest of her life campaigning against social injustice and the oppression of women.

Anna wiped her eyes and turned away. She knew in her heart that one chapter in her life had ended. Though she had experienced heartache and loneliness in Siam, she had also learned a great deal. But the West was calling, as was Anna's maternal instinct. She longed for the day when their ship would dock in England and she could hold her beloved Avis in her arms again.

Anna never returned to the fabled kingdom.

Chapter 3
On to America

It's never easy leaving behind the familiar and taking one's first steps into the unknown. But then Anna never let fears of the unknown stop her from doing anything. During the long voyage to England, she had ample time to reflect on how the years in the Siamese court had taken their toll.

Anna was beset by maternal longings as the ship drew closer to Europe's shores. Avis would now be a young lady, 14 years old, who had grown up in a school in England. Anna sighed as she thought how difficult it must have been for Avis to adjust to a new life in cold, damp England after the heat and warmth of life in the East. She thought about how Avis must have pined away the long, dull evenings when the thin British rain drizzled on the windows of her dormitory, and comforted herself by thinking that it was for Avis's benefit that she had been sent away. Nevertheless, there had been many nights in the sultry Bangkok heat that Anna had not been able to sleep because she was thinking about her absent daughter. On these occasions she would rise, wrapping a gown about her, and sit for long hours at the window staring vainly into the dark for some measure of peace. Longing for her daughter had been with her every day.

As the ship neared the coast of England on a cold and foggy morning, Anna looked out of the porthole and saw the faint outline of land in the distance. It cheered her, and despite the uncomfortable clamminess in the cabin, Anna felt her heart beating joyously. Avis would be waiting. Louis was still asleep and rolled back and forth as the ship pitched on the choppy waters. Anna quickly shook him awake and together they stared out into the clearing horizon as if they could already see Avis.

Anna had, to this point, lived most of her life in the East and the cold dampness of England hit her like a fist when she stepped ashore. There was a tremendous din around her. Somewhat confused, she and Louis stood for a few minutes, surrounded by their baggage. Louis had been dreading the final outcome of this voyage. His mother was thinking about that, too, and struggled to smother her emotions. They both knew it would soon be his turn to be enrolled in a boarding school, and Louis was not relishing the prospect of a dull, strict routine. Seagulls screamed and swooped as

Anna clutched her handbag with one hand, while holding on tightly to her son with the other. Her eyes searched desperately among the crowds. Porters repeatedly asked her if she required help, and street urchins ran around with red cheeks and tattered clothes, begging for coins. Suddenly, Anna drew a deep breath and then a gentle calmness settled over her. She had spotted Avis among the crowd. There she was, a young girl with a slim figure, huge brown eyes, and a straight back, scanning the new arrivals and looking rather desperate. It could only be Avis. With another deep breath, Anna pulled Louis towards her and waved, calling her daughter's name.

Soon mother and daughter were locked in a tight embrace, eyes wet, and faces beaming. At first Louis found it comical, but he was soon caught up in the emotion of it all as his older sister hugged him. The reunited family left the docks and drove across London in a hansom cab (a two-wheeled vehicle pulled by two horses), which was piled high with their luggage. The cab driver must have been bemused by the unrestrained exclamations and laughter he heard from within.

Anna had already arranged for rented rooms and Anna, Avis, and Louis moved in together, happy at least for a while, to be a family again. Anna spent some of the most delightful days of her life during this time. Together they toured the city, taking in the sights and sounds of the London that Avis knew so well, linking hands wherever they went, talking and laughing. They sat on the grass in Hyde Park, strolled around

Trafalgar Square, and fed the pigeons. Louis and his mother told Avis about the fantastic royal court in Bangkok, the saffron-robed monks, and the giant Reclining Buddha.

Avis told them of her experiences living in a boarding school, which struck terror in Louis's heart. He was not looking forward to the end of these joyous days when he would have to go off to a boarding school that emphasized book learning and development of character. After the carefree life he had led in the royal palace at Bangkok, it seemed impossible that he could ever be happy in an enclosed setting. He recalled how he used to wake up every morning to his pet parrot nibbling on his ear, then race off to the pond nearby to join the other town boys, who were splashing wildly about in the water. This invigorating activity was followed by a breakfast of fruit and milk, after which he would play with his neighbourhood friends until his mother was ready to go to the palace. They usually journeyed by rickshaw and boat to arrive at the huge gates of the palace. There the sentries would salute smartly as they walked into the compound. Louis always had a sense of coming home when he entered the palace. He told Avis how the royal classroom had fresh flowers every day and huge meals of the most delicious food he had ever eaten. Louis waved his hands in animation, and his expressive eyes were alight as he told her stories of his time with his best friend, Prince Chulalongkorn. In the beginning, he related, he was a little shy with the prince, but that was only because he was unsure of how to behave with a king's son and wondered whether he was expected to bow every time the prince spoke or looked at him. That would have been difficult, he informed Avis gravely, because the prince usually had such a mischievous look, as if he were about to burst into laughter. Anna added that the two boys were certainly a handful, and that in the classroom she had made them sit apart from each other because they were always getting into mischief together.

Anna was well aware of Louis's feelings about boarding school. She knew that he was apprehensive, but being a strict disciplinarian, she was also aware that the lax and luxurious life that was the routine at the royal palace was unnatural. They were not of royal blood, and those days would have come to an end under any circumstances. It was better, she reasoned, for Louis to get a dose of reality. Louis would have to make his own way in the world. For this eventuality, a sense of discipline and a good education were mandatory. Anna desperately hoped that he would see that those carefree days in Bangkok were over and come to understand why. She hardened her heart because she knew that just as she had managed to send Avis away, she must do the same with Louis.

Anna was always conscious that she was the sole guardian of her children and that she was all that stood between them and anarchy. She rarely looked back at her own childhood because it caused her too much pain and uneasiness. But Anna knew that what she had lacked in her life as a child was a sense of purpose and discipline, and she was determined that her children would grow up with a sense of responsibility and independence. Amid much flinching and sobbing, Anna steeled herself to put Louis on a coach bound for Dublin. Her late husband's relatives would meet him in Dublin and take him to the school. But after he had left, Anna was conscious of an unending pain in her breast. Why did her children have to be separated from her? First Avis and now Louis, whose absence had already created another enormous gap in her life. Mother and daughter tried to comfort each other through this difficult time, and they vowed that they would never be separated again.

It was nearing autumn in England. Mist swirled about the house and dampness invaded every bone in Anna's body. With a constant cough and aching joints, Anna began to long for the heat of the East. Quite suddenly she was filled with a desire to escape the fog-ridden evenings. Depression became a frequent companion and Anna considered the pros and cons of returning to Siam with Avis. The king had granted her a six-month leave and it was almost up. But as Anna reviewed her situation, she began to realize that her salary had been inadequate in view of the amount of work she was expected to do. She decided to write to the king and state her case. It was possible that he would increase her salary or perhaps lessen her workload. After all, she had been doing the work of two separate people, she grumbled to Avis. She was the governess and the secretary to the king. Surely it was not unfair on her part to expect more?

Winter was now settling in and Anna had begun to reassess her life. Louis wrote long letters bursting with rancour and rage. His anger resonated with homesickness as he railed at his mother for depositing him in the boarding school. Poor Louis was finding the bonds of discipline very limiting. The anguished letters continued.

Many weeks later, Anna received a reply from King Mongkut, but her excitement quickly turned to irritation. Though she had clearly asked for a raise, the king had been vague, and instead of a higher salary he had offered her a £200 loan. Anna did not want a loan. She was weary at the thought of working day and night again. Many times she imagined herself back in Bangkok, translating documents or writing letters and then trying to find the energy to face the next day and teach. For many a long evening after, Anna paced the wooden floors of their new home, with Avis looking on. Should she reply to the king's letter indicating she was ready to return to Bangkok? Peering through the windowpanes of her rooms in England, Anna saw the mist and the dripping yews in the empty street. Sighing, she turned away, drawing her shawl tightly around her and taking care to cover her chronically sore throat.

As Anna looked around the room, her eyes fell on an unopened letter from Dr. Francis Cobb, and her irritation began to dissipate. She had met the kind doctor while married to Leon in Singapore. A gust of sorrow tempered her pleasure as she touched the stiff white envelope, her husband had been alive then ... and Anna remembered life being vastly different. What days those were!

Sighing, she asked Avis if she remembered Dr. Cobb. Avis had never forgotten the kind doctor who visited so often when her father was alive. Dr. Cobb seemed like their link with that time. But after Leon's death, a strain had arisen between them — it was not seemly for the doctor to continue visiting Anna and the children as he had earlier. There were always people who gossiped and pointed fingers, so Dr. Cobb tactfully refrained from calling alone, and they had to be content with the occasional exchange of a few words in church. A few weeks after Leon's death they had gone their separate ways, but the warmth of friendship and a common interest in humanity made it seem as if the intervening years were but yesterday. Just before Anna and Louis left for Siam, Dr. Cobb called to bid them goodbye, a gesture that had deeply moved Anna. He was one of the few who genuinely supported her decision and applauded her courage. They had stayed in touch over the years, continuing to discuss books and ideas through their letters.

Dr. Cobb was an American, a learned man with humanistic values and a passion for his country. The idea of slavery was anathema to Dr. Cobb, and he argued passionately against the enslavement of one human being by another. He embodied the best of Yankee idealism and epitomized the values of human dignity and freedom from oppression. Anna could not help being influenced by such high ideals.

They had spent many an evening in stimulating discussion. With the children playing by his side, Dr. Cobb would tell them about the latest book he had read. He often discussed authors like Nathaniel Hawthorne, Ralph Waldo Emerson, and Harriet Beecher Stowe. He sometimes read aloud from Stowe's *Uncle Tom's Cabin*, in his deep and sonorous voice. Soon, even the children and Leon would be immersed in the tale of the heroine who so captured their imagination. Anna was particularly struck by a quote from Stowe's writing, "It's a matter of taking the side of the weak against the strong, something the best people have always done." While in Siam, she had often read from *Uncle Tom's Cabin*, which left an indelible impression on many of her Siamese students.

Tearing open the envelope, she told Avis that she was going to feel cheerful soon. Dr. Cobb's letters always gave her food for thought. The letter inquired warmly about her well being and the children's. He was writing to say that he was now married to a woman named Katherine, whom he had met in Singapore. He was at the end of his service in the Orient and was returning to America. He hoped Anna would honour him and Katherine with a visit in their new home. Anna felt her heart leap; a path had suddenly opened up before her. It would be perfect, she told Avis, as she excitedly paced the floor. They would go and see America, the land where people made their fortunes and wrote their own histories, where old conventions that had bound people and limited their potential were simply cast aside. There, you carved out your own destiny. Your personal values were what guided you, not archaic ideas about class and race. Avis sat watching her mother's animated face. It didn't matter to Avis where they went, as long as they were together.

Anna paused suddenly. She had momentarily forgotten that she would have to tell Louis. She wondered how he would take the news. Surely, he would be willing to quit his boarding school and follow them across the Atlantic and, for a moment, she was tempted. They would be together again and he would cease sending her those heart-wrenching letters. But then, she shook her head determinedly; Louis was better off where he was. She would have to harden her heart one more time.

As they had their dinner that night, Anna pondered the doctor's words. She told Avis about slavery and the Civil War that was fought over it, and she recalled how she used to shudder as Dr. Cobb narrated harrowing tales of life on southern plantations. It was a glorious cause. In the flickering candlelight, Anna grabbed the writing paper and began a long letter to Dr. Cobb and Katherine. She thanked them for their kind offer and said she was seriously considering visiting them in America. Anna went to bed that night with a light heart. Her dreams were full of runaway slaves, vast stretches of water, and women fighting for their rights.

At about that same time, Anna received news that King Mongkut had died and that Prince Chulalongkorn had ascended the throne. She wrote a letter of condolence to the prince and asked if he required her services. Though part of her wanted to experience the new life in America, another part of her knew she would not mind returning to Bangkok on her own terms. The dilemma was resolved for her in an unexpected fashion. The prince replied, thanking her for the condolence message. However, there was no mention of her return. Anna realized that the door had closed.

True to her nature, she abruptly began to focus on the possibility of a visit to America and a new beginning. The next morning, Anna told Avis that they were going to visit Dr. Cobb and make a new life in America. Avis knew her mother's determination well by now, and she was not at all unhappy about the idea. The young teen's only need was the security of her mother's love. It didn't matter to her whether they lived in England or New York.

As they waited for Dr. Cobb to reply and set a tentative date for their travel, Anna told Avis about the anti-slavery activists. Her blood boiled while she told Avis stories of atrocities committed against slaves. Anna fervently believed that slavery was morally and ethically wrong. In Siam, she had taken every opportunity to stand up for the rights of the oppressed. Whenever she witnessed an abuse of power or an injustice, Anna had not been able to keep quiet. Even if it was the king himself who was the abuser, she had made her opinion known. The downtrodden had always engaged her sympathy. For years Anna had been, unknowingly, developing her gift of being able to see the extent of a problem and envision a solution. This gift would come in useful later in her life as an activist.

As they prepared to leave, Anna opened her trunk and carefully removed the emerald ring. Avis was dazzled by the glitter of the stone set in gold. Anna told Avis the story of the ring. She described how Hidden Perfume had been so taken by *Uncle Tom's Cabin* that she announced that, thereafter, she was going to be known as "Harriet Beecher Stowe Son Klin."

Anna felt that she had come to a crossroads in her life. She was now ready to go to a land where there was the promise of freedom from class distinction. She longed to see the country where the people in the north were prepared to go to war against their own countrymen in the south, because they believed in human dignity and morality and did not believe in slavery. It seemed to her that she would fit right into that society.

Mother and daughter awaited Dr. Cobb's response with eagerness. He and his wife had already arrived and had set up their home near Boston. They extended a warm welcome to Anna and Avis, promising them a good holiday. Despite Louis's protests and fears, Anna and Avis boarded a ship for their transatlantic voyage. It was almost the end of winter by the time they reached Boston. Spring was in the air and the sense of a new beginning was overpowering in Anna. She leaned over the ship's rails, waiting to catch a glimpse of Dr. Cobb and his bride. Everything was so new and so exciting, she later told the doctor with a laugh, that she felt reborn.

The next few months with the Cobbs were stimulating for Anna in many ways, because their hosts made her and Avis feel truly welcome in their home. In the bracing climate, among friends, Anna blossomed. As in times past, she and the doctor spent many hours discussing the effects of slavery on human beings, what it did to the human psyche, and why this social evil must be rooted out.

Many of the Cobbs's friends visited regularly, and Anna created a minor sensation with accounts of her experiences at the Siamese court. Suddenly, she realized that she had captured people's imaginations in a big way. She told the story of Hidden Perfume and proudly showed the emerald ring on her finger. To those who lived circumscribed lives without opportunities to travel the world, she was a godsend. They would listen, spellbound, to her stories of her years of palace life in Siam. Most of her new acquaintances were amazed that a widow with young children would have the courage to do such a thing. They marvelled at her and sought her out for a constant round of parties and talks, eager to hear her eloquent narrations. Her talent for bringing her tales to life through detail and exaggeration was obvious. Over time, her stories grew more and more vivid, the characters more sharply etched, the emotions magnified to huge proportions.

It was an invigorating time, but eventually, Anna grew troubled as reality set in. Although being with the Cobbs had been good for partially regaining her health, her finances were not at all healthy. In fact, they had dwindled alarmingly. She knew they could not stay on with the kind doctor and his wife for much longer. So, after much thought and worry, they bid the Cobbs a reluctant goodbye, and Anna and her daughter travelled up to the Catskill Mountains, away from the city. There they rented rooms in a modest lodge and lived quietly, keeping to themselves, while Anna thought about her next step. Visitors to the wilderness region often saw Anna's tall aristocratic figure marching through the forests of spruce, pine, basswood, and white birch. They speculated about who she might be. Some whispered that perhaps she was a princess, fleeing from the pressures of a royal home.

The remote mountain air also proved beneficial for Anna's physical health and she began to feel better than she had in a very long time. Yet, emotionally, Anna was not healing. Louis wrote desperate letters to her — he did not want to continue in the boarding school. He told her that the strict discipline and the school's narrowness confined his spirit, and he listed the reasons why his mother would need him when she retuned to Siam. Anna had frequently struggled with her conscience on this. Finally, she let Louis know that there would be no return to Siam.

At this point, Anna's immediate concern was money. Now, without a regular income, it was imperative that she think of a way to support her family. Once again, she had to face this problem alone. But she had already proved that she could earn her own living. She had even had the audacity to work for a king. Surely she could find a way. New York City was not far away, and Anna, with typical resourcefulness, decided to try her luck there. She had heard stories about how the city had been moulded by immigrants, and she was confident that she might be able to make a decent living in New York. When her mind was firmly made up, she told Avis they were going to New York to set up their home. Anna was sure that where there were immigrants from all over the world, there must be a need for teachers.

Staten Island, New York, was a bustling city, vigorous with new immigrants. They came off the boats in large numbers, eager to pursue their destinies. Young men, older men with families, and women with children thronged into the city looking for work. Anna set up home and immediately began planning her livelihood. By this time, the state of their finances was becoming critical. She advertised in the papers and eventually, she and Avis, who was now a young woman, opened a school for children. By day Anna and Avis worked long hours in an effort to build a reputation for their school. Gradually, their financial situation began to improve, but it was slow going and their circumstances remained precarious for some time.

In the evenings, they went for long walks. There were vast stretches of open parkland and wide-mouthed rivers teeming with fish and wildlife in the forests beyond. Anna loved the outdoors and firmly believed that exercise produced healthy bodies and minds. One day, while they were walking, Avis came up with an idea that she felt might improve their situation. She pointed out that Anna was a talented storyteller. Avis believed that if her mother began to put her stories down on paper, readers would lap them up. Perhaps her mother could write about her experiences at the Siamese court, Avis reasoned. Few people in the United States even knew about Siam, let alone had ever met a real king. Stories like this would be welcomed and sought after by the public.

Anna sat down on a log in a clearing in the woods. Her heart was beating fast and her face was flushed from brisk walking. She considered the matter seriously. It was true that whenever she spoke to people about her life at the Siamese court, they were fascinated, listening open-mouthed at the strange ways of the royal household. Avis reminded her that Dr. Cobb's guests had always shown a great deal of interest in her stories. If she could tell the stories and keep people spellbound, then the same thing would likely happen if she put these fascinating stories in a book. Once Anna considered all the pros and cons, she decided that she would try her hand at writing. If nothing else, she told Avis, she could at least take a shot at writing an article or two.

After Anna and Avis became established in New York and had somewhat recovered financially, they once again began to circulate socially. At one gathering, Anna met a young man named Thomas Fyshe, a Scotsman who was a banker. She took an immediate liking to the serious-minded young man and invited him over to their house the next day. While they were having tea, Anna noticed that Avis and Thomas seemed to be attracted to each other. Avis was a beautiful and gracious young woman with her mother's remarkable brown eyes and tall figure. Anna sensed that there was something solid about Thomas Fyshe and Avis seemed to find this comforting. Anna waited patiently for things to fall into place.

In the meantime, Anna was beginning to realize that, in order to continue supporting her children, she would need more income than her little school could generate. Remembering Avis's words, she wrote some articles about her Siam experiences and submitted them to *Atlantic Monthly*. James Freeman Clarke, the editor of the magazine, was struck by the personal touch in her writing, and to Anna's surprise and excitement, the articles were accepted. Once Clarke realized how popular the pieces were, he asked for four more. He encouraged Anna to continue to write about what she had seen in Siam, explaining that the readers of the *Atlantic Monthly* were clamouring for the exotic true-life tales. It was a shot in the arm for Anna. The articles brought her not only money but also, gradually, a reputation. Anna knew then that the time was ripe for serious writing.

Soon, Anna had enough material to expand her original articles into a book. Upon completion of *The English Governess in the Siamese Court: Recollections of Six Years at the Royal Palace at Bangkok* in 1870, she immediately began a second book. Through each long evening and late into the night, Anna wove her tales, which she creatively sprinkled with exotic details. Slowly, she began to make her name in literary circles, and Anna soon found herself accepting offers to lecture about her experiences to fascinated and information-hungry audiences. Anna really was a born storyteller, and her presence, her cultivated speaking voice, and her confident demeanour attracted a vast array of people.

By 1872, Anna was touring the United States as a much sought-after literary personality. Everywhere, she was met by adoring readers, and before she knew it, she was moving in different social and professional circles altogether. Other well-known writers such as Oliver Wendell Holmes, Ralph Waldo Emerson, Henry Wadsworth Longfellow, and Julia Ward Holmes became her contemporaries and friends. A special place in Anna's heart had always been reserved for Harriet Beecher Stowe, whom Anna finally had an opportunity to meet during her North American tour.

Her second book, *The Romance of the Harem* (1873), was based on two of her *Atlantic Monthly* articles, "Favourite of the Harem" and "L'Ore: The Slave of the Siamese Queen." Such sensationalism was rare in the book world in that era. As she watched her work being bought up by her eager readers, she realized the public had an insatiable appetite for her writing. Anna grew increasingly more confident of her ability to captivate readers.

Meanwhile, while Anna was touring and lecturing, Thomas Fyshe proposed to Avis. After a happy courtship and with Anna's blessing, the two were married in New York in 1878. Anna was thrilled, but was overwhelmed with long-forgotten memories as Avis walked down the aisle. Anna felt a lump in her throat and her eyes grew moist with tears as she thought back to her own wedding with a twist in her heart. It was all so long ago, another age almost, and much had changed. Anna was well aware that she herself had changed tremendously. From a wide-eyed little barracks girl she had grown into a sophisticated woman of the world, an author and a sought-after speaker. Images from the past coursed before her as she sat in the pew: Avis at six months in a rest house in the wilds of interior India ... Avis weeping at her father's deathbed ... Avis's small face growing smaller and smaller as the ship bound for England moved away from the dock. Anna sighed and clutched her hands tightly. It would not do to become emotional in public. Avis was lucky to have Thomas. The young couple was very much in love. Anna hoped that Avis's husband would prove to be a little more assertive in marriage than her Leon had been. She felt that Avis needed a decisive man around the house. Anna knew just how burdensome it was for a woman to raise her children and to take on the role of head of the household, as well.

As the organ played, Anna's thoughts flew over the ocean to Louis. He had grown up, finished boarding school, and had returned to the Orient to find work. Anna wished he had more of a purpose in life — his main interest seemed to be having a good time. Despite her hopes and dreams for Louis, boarding school had not made him into the kind of man Anna had hoped. He seemed lackadaisical and was too fond of the good things in life. Perhaps, Anna thought with regret, he had never grown up after they left Siam. Louis seemed to continue in his own dream world. He was incurably fascinated with the Orient and it was obvious that he shunned the everyday business of life. Anna had tried to convince him to settle down in America, but he was clearly not interested. Sadly, Louis never did come back to her and Avis.

When Avis and Thomas left for their honeymoon Anna spent the time alone, fervently writing. She continued to think back on her life and the lives of her children. Around that time she received a letter from Louis and read with a heavy heart that he was working in Australia. As only a mother can, Anna prayed that he would be happy doing whatever it was he wanted to do.

Avis and Thomas returned from their honeymoon and set up their home not far from Anna's house. It was obvious that Avis could not bear to be apart from Anna for long. Fortunately, Thomas knew their history and he did not seem to mind. The two women spent many afternoons together discussing experiences, mishaps, Anna's writing, and everything else under the sun, and growing closer than ever together. They often talked about Louis and Avis gradually began to realize that she was the only person whom her mother could call her own. Avis had known all along that her brother would never come back to them. Nevertheless,

On to America

Anna, Avis, and Thomas were happy in their lives, got along well with each other, and passed their days and evenings in each other's company. Both Anna and Thomas were of strong temperament, but they respected each other's viewpoints and each other's singleness of purpose.

Anna was becoming more and more famous with each passing year. There were frequent invitations to lecture about her experiences in the Orient, and she travelled all over the United States sharing her knowledge. Her talks were always well attended, partly because of her commanding presence and partly because of her ever-fascinating subject matter.

Chapter 4
Life in Canada — From Author to Activist

L ife took an interesting turn for the family later that year when Thomas was offered a job up north in Canada. The Bank of Nova Scotia in Halifax had made Thomas a tempting offer, and for several days he debated his best course of action. Should he move to Canada? It would be a bold move. Anna and Avis, with great trepidation, waited patiently for Thomas to make this very important decision. When he finally did decide, Thomas and Avis asked Anna to move with them to Halifax. Avis had told Thomas, tearfully, that she could not bear the thought of separation from her mother.

Anna thought about the move and then enthusiastically agreed to the plan. Louis seemed to be settled in Australia, where he had spent the previous four years. Knowing this, Anna was quite willing to set up home in a new land, too. Anna's wanderlust had never really left her — and Canada was a real frontier. As the day approached for their move, Anna began to look forward to a new life with considerable enthusiasm. As she bid goodbye to her admirers and friends in New York, Anna arranged to continue her work from Nova Scotia, confident that Canada would offer her new opportunities.

Halifax was a garrison city. Known as the peninsular province of Canada, it was filled with fun and abandon for the military elite stationed there, a far cry from the garrison towns Anna remembered. The family of three set out on a tour of Halifax shortly after they arrived. First, they visited the Citadel, a magnificent star-shaped fortress on top of a huge hill that looks down at the sprawling city's dramatic coastline. Prince Edward, who at the time was the commander-in-chief of Nova Scotia, had built the heavily armed garrison. Their guide informed them that a clock tower had been added to the Citadel in 1803.

Anna, Avis, and Thomas walked down to the busy harbour to watch the unloading of sailing ships from all over the world. Strolling along the harbour, where the gulls wheeled and swooped, Anna pointed out to Avis that it was entirely possible that one of the ships in the harbour had come from as far away as Siam, and maybe even Australia. They noticed the many merchantmen and seamen on Halifax's streets, many of whom wore colourful clothes and large earrings.

Seafarers had a long history in Halifax, and it was common for many generations of one family to be connected to the sea in some way. Anna, Thomas, and Avis spent considerable time admiring the great ships that stood tall in the water. The year was 1878, the era of the great wooden ships, and these golden years of sail and shipbuilding in Halifax played a major part in the economy of Nova Scotia.

In their initial months in Halifax, Anna and Avis took great delight in what became a daily exploration of this fascinating city, so Victorian in appearance and character. Anna especially liked touring the English forts around the city, which never ceased to remind her of Poona and the brave princess who defended the ancient fort on the hill. This great city by the sea quickly captured their hearts, and the family settled into a home in a well-established area of the city, the North West Arm, which was known for its natural charm and beauty, as well as for its illustrious residents.

Anna Leonowens had arrived in Halifax preceded by her reputation as an author and lecturer, and its citizens were eager to meet her. As the family gradually got to know the city's inhabitants, Anna began to make her presence felt. She was invited to join various committees and causes, and her social consciousness continued to escalate. Her son-in-law's connections in the upper strata of Halifax society ensured that she met a mix of well-educated people who had both influence and wealth. This was a stimulating time for Anna, as her new acquaintances were anxious to hear her views on slavery and oppression. She was passionate about this subject and her drawing room at the Fyshe home soon became a meeting ground for new projects and for the exchange of ideas.

Ever since her days in Siam, Anna had been interested in the arts. This particular period of Victorian Halifax marked the development of amateur theatre and many local societies produced shows that were enthusiastically welcomed by Haligonians. Anna and Avis always attended these events, and she often thought back, wistfully, to the theatrical events she had attended with Louis, so many years past in the Siamese court.

Revitalized, Anna wasted no time in energetically diving into the thick of things. She founded a weekly Shakespeare club, at which men and women met and read Shakespeare. Anna thoroughly enjoyed this add-on to her education. Her love of learning continued to increase with the years, and she discovered a new appreciation for the arts. Apart from theatricals, Halifax offered numerous sporting activities, and Anna and her family and friends often attended aquatic carnivals, curling bonspiels, yacht races, and tennis competitions.

But not all Haligonians led this kind of life. Caught up in the continuous upper-class frenzy of social events, it was some time before it dawned on Anna how the other half lived. Then, slowly but surely, the realization of social inequality began to filter into her consciousness. It began when she started accompanying a household servant to the market. Tradesmen hawked hard-boiled gull eggs and lobsters in wooden barrels, and merchants who dressed in exotic clothes and jewellery filled the streets. What Anna saw was colourful, no doubt, but she also noticed the underlying poverty, hunger, and grime. A great number of grim-looking characters roamed the streets. Children as young as nine and ten played unsupervised around the marketplace. Anna, who had once lived like this herself, sensed an overwhelming desperation and hopelessness. She began to read disturbing articles in the local newspaper and learned that in some parts of the city, especially the seedier district where the barracks were, women were often arrested for being inebriated.

Anna picked up threads of conversation among the ladies at the evening teas, who whispered in hushed tones about the horrors of life for the denizens of the lower rungs of society. In the elegant drawing rooms of the rich, the women gossiped about the degradation their unfortunate sisters were subjected to, which seemed to have a number of causes — poverty, illiteracy, alcohol, and disease foremost among them. By this time Anna had become deeply concerned about society's treatment of women, and she firmly believed that it was possible to raise the status of these unfortunate women through social action.

While she was in the United States, she had taken part in many anti-slavery demonstrations and had heard, with increasing compassion, stories of the lives of the unfortunate. Slavery had not taken root in Nova Scotia as it had in the United States and, although locals referred to the black community as the "slave society," there were no plantations in the province. The British had promised 100-acre land grants to loyalist blacks that agreed to fight against the Americans, but these grants had never materialized. The black population was left to fend for themselves and make do with hard, stony land. They were victims of prejudice and discrimination and were excluded from the almost-wholly-white schools, churches, and social organizations. The slums of Africville on the outskirts of Halifax were shocking.

Anna was increasingly aware of the full extent of Halifax's social problems. What particularly captured her attention was that the lower-class women in Halifax were considered the dregs of humanity, just as they had been back in India, in garrison towns like Poona. Anna was adamant that she was not going to sit by and continue to let this happen. Some of the ladies who met at the evening soirees had become her friends and they felt as strongly about the issue as she did. Anna pointed out that the situation was not just a local one; injustice and a lack of basic human rights afflicted women all over the world. She often related the story of Tuptim, a young girl in the Siamese court who fell in love with a monk and wanted nothing more than to serve him. The king eventually had the two of them put to death. Anna described the dungeons where the unfortunate Tuptim was imprisoned during the trial — and the Halifax ladies were speechless with horror. Anna felt that the only way to liberate women from oppression was to educate them and provide them with a sense of self-worth and the means to gain economic independence. That, she predicted, would come about only with activism.

In the 1880s, ideas slowly began to ferment about the social condition of women. Anna and her friends and acquaintances were beginning to examine the basis of their privileged lives and to question themselves about their own duties and priorities. Since they were so privileged, should they not act for the betterment of those less fortunate? Anna remembered that during one of her lecture tours in the United States, after the publication of her second book, *The Romance of the Harem*, she was enthusiastically questioned by women in the audience who wanted to know what they could do to help their sisters.

In Toronto, there were already stirrings of what was eventually referred to as "the women's movement." The reports reached Halifax and were eagerly read by the ladies in Anna's circle. Emily Stowe, Anna's long-time role model, had founded the Toronto Women's Suffrage Association in 1883. Its members addressed the conditions affecting women at the time, and spoke out about how their personal lives contradicted their professional lives and created a gap that was impossible to close. Stowe's speeches on "women's sphere" and "women in the professions" had a great impact on Anna. For example, Stowe, finding it impossible to get a medical education in Canada, was forced to study at the New York Medical College for Women. When she returned to Canada, hoping to set up a practice specializing in the ailments of women and children, the College of Physicians and Surgeons of Ontario refused to give her a medical licence. Not to be deterred, she practiced medicine in Ontario for some time without a local licence. Stowe campaigned relentlessly for the right of women to be doctors and, ultimately, she received her licence to practice in Ontario. Finally, in 1883, the Ontario Medical College for Women became a reality, largely due to Stowe's efforts.

It was impossible not to be influenced and excited by these early strides in achieving equal rights for the women of Canada. Anna's days and evenings were filled with concerted efforts to improve conditions for women in Nova Scotia. The desperate lives of those living on Albermarle and Barrack Streets, the lives of servitude and degradation of the inhabitants of Africville, and the wretched condition of women in the labour market chafed at Anna's sensibilities. She put all her efforts into helping them.

While Anna was fighting this new cause, Avis was having one child after another, to the delight of her husband and mother. When Anna held her first granddaughter, who was (not surprisingly) named Ann, she promised to fight tooth and nail to uphold the rights of this tiny precious person. Anna vowed that her little Ann would not be disadvantaged because of her gender.

Anna also remained active on other fronts throughout the 1880s, continuing to write books and articles. In 1881, she received a letter from the prestigious magazine, *The Youth's*

Companion, which had been published in Boston since 1827. Willa Cather, Mark Twain, O. Henry, Emily Dickinson, Francis Scott Key, and Winston Churchill had all contributed to the magazine over time. The editor of the action and adventure section asked Anna if she was interested in a reporting assignment in a remote part of the world. The magazine wanted a series of articles about the common people in Russia following the great upheaval that occurred when Czar Alexander II faced opposition from various factions within the empire.

When Avis heard about the offer, she was aghast that her mother would even consider it. The entire country was aflame with internal and volatile crises. Who knew what dangers awaited anyone foolhardy enough to venture there? Anna calmed Avis down by pointing out that there were others, male journalists, who were extremely keen to go and that the editor would have doubts about sending a woman to tackle the wilds of Siberia. Avis began to relax.

A short time later, news filtered out of Russia that, on March 13, 1881, Nihilists in St. Petersburg had assassinated Alexander. Avis was absolutely certain that Anna would no longer consider the offer under these conditions. It was madness to contemplate going at this juncture! However, the magazine's management believed that a mature woman travelling alone in Russia, especially in the aftermath of the Czar's assassination, would be at an advantage. The assignment required a unique blend of courage and common sense, and Anna's lively imagination, her success as an author and lecturer, and her earlier global adventures all combined to convince them that Anna Leonowens was the right choice. Avis was horrified. The offer was a great boost for Anna, but once again, friends and family warned her against taking up the challenge.

In the end, Anna's unquenchable thirst for the unknown influenced her final decision. There were other Victorian women who had traversed far-off corners of the globe to climb the Himalayas, to search for botanical specimens in North and South America, to work with missionaries in India and Tibet, and to ford rushing rivers in the Americas. Anna was among those who ventured outside the strict physical boundaries that the Victorians drew around their womenfolk. In 1881, at the age of 49, Anna set sail for Russia. She mollified Avis by telling her that two armed guards had been contracted to protect her as she crossed the Russian steppes.

As soon as she arrived, Anna and her bodyguards set out across the country. Covered with quilts, blankets, and furs, Anna perched uncomfortably on a sled in the half-light of a Russian evening. (Most of her travel was by horse sled as the Trans-Siberian Railway was still 11 years away from being built.) She shifted restlessly in her seat, which was nothing more than a straw-covered box that held her provisions, and drew her rough quilt closely around her as the horses ploughed relentlessly through the deep snow. The sled driver sang out coarsely, his voice echoing and warbling drunkenly through the forest trails. He took frequent gulps of vodka and Anna began to wonder if they would ever reach the post house, their first night's destination. Dark trees with icicles on their boughs loomed by the wayside and most of the roadway was frozen. Anna held on tight, thoroughly absorbed in the mystery and glamour of the fast-approaching night. Somewhere in the forest a wolf howled, and his brothers immediately took up his cry.

By the time she reached the post house, her body was aching from the extreme cold and the continuous jolting. The small log cabin had huge roaring samovars (metal urns with taps used to boil water for tea) in the corners. Families were cooking their meals and warming up soup and tea to fortify them against the bitter cold. Their sheepskin rugs steamed and the smell arising from them was appalling. Anna took a little time to get used to her surroundings. Then she took off her felt boots and overshoes, her eiderdown coat, and her sheepskin overcoat and laid them out carefully to dry. She patted her greying hair in place and sat down primly to inspect her neighbours. Her bodyguards were snoring in a corner after consuming enormous amounts of vodka and stale bread. Picking at her bread, Anna held a bowl of very hot ragout close to her body. Its delicious combination of crayfish, crabs, and vegetables soothed her and gave her the energy she needed to begin a letter to Avis. From then on, every evening after the day's travelling was done, Anna recorded the day's events in her diary and wrote letters to her daughter. The Russian scenery was so varied and the customs so quaint that it was easy for Anna to write lengthy missives to her family. In addition, she kept copious notes in preparation for her series of articles for the magazine. She wanted her readers to be able to picture the life of an average Russian against the backdrop of political upheaval.

Anna was sympathetic to the lot of the common people, and the women in particular. While travelling about in the cities, she focused her attention on the female students who were bent on gaining an education and qualifying as teachers. Her feminist heart was roused by stories of these brave young women who were commonly denied easy access to education because of their gender. Knowing first-hand how education broadens the mind and how she herself had struggled to obtain admission into the ranks of the educated, Anna felt a sense of oneness with these Russian women.

The roads between the cities and towns led to small hamlets that, with spring approaching, boasted a wild and untamed beauty. Forests of pine, fir, birch, aspen, and larch covered mile after mile. Anna's heart soared at the sight of flower-filled meadows ringed by pristine lakes. There were wild ducks on the lakes and the fields burst with sweet peas. Whenever possible, and if the foggy morning was not too cold, she took her tea by the side of a log house. Looking out towards the clear waters of the lakes, Anna sampled the delicious local confit: pork, duck, goose, or turkey, which was cooked slowly, preserved in its own fat, and then mixed with huckleberries. After each day of passing through deep canyons and misty valleys, Anna would enthusiastically begin writing. Sometimes she gazed, transfixed for long periods of time, at the high mountains, which reminded her of the Himalayas. The Volga River and the central agricultural areas through which she passed gave her many glimpses of the peasants who seemed oblivious to the happenings in the city, and to the political upheaval that was threatening the lives of so many Russians in towns and cities. The lives of the peasants were one long continuous struggle from one season to the next as they toiled to feed and raise their children.

Slowly the weather improved as the spring thaw set in. Though the hummingbirds flitting over roadside raspberry bushes were a charming sight, they now had to contend with swarms of mosquitoes from the shifting bogs and marshes. Dust got into her clothes, her skin, and her hair. Travel at this time of year was sometimes by barge and sometimes by carriage. Frequently, the sky clouded over and a torrential rain descended, soaking the travellers, who were often forced to seek shelter in the huts of nearby peasants.

Anna met and talked with many mountain people during her journey. They showered her with rustic hospitality and showed her their small well-tended vegetable gardens. In the summer, the peasants generally made their homes in cone-shaped birchbark tents, which were made of a base of larch wood cut into narrow slats and covered with birchbark and horsehair. The biggest advantage to these shelters was that there were no mosquitoes inside. The matriarch of each household, dressed in a short leather jacket and thick boots with voluminous petticoats, usually offered Anna a bowl of *kumyss* (a refreshing drink made of mare's milk). The peasant would pick a cabbage and a few potatoes from his garden in honour of his guest. Anna never forgot the warm welcome these poor peasants gave her in this strange and far-away land. Each time she took leave of her hosts, she would give the children small packets of tea and sugar, which were received with squeals of joy.

After passing through the foothills of the mountains, which were aflame with ripe wild strawberries, Anna at last entered the bustling city of Moscow. In addition to the Russian language, Moscow's vibrant and sophisticated inhabitants spoke fluent French and German. The latest fashionable hats and gowns adorned the refined women who surrounded Anna when she attended services in St. Basil's Cathedral. Though not overtly religious, Anna was smitten by the grand architecture of the cathedral. Built by Ivan the Terrible in the famous Red Square, with its distinctive domes and nine chapels, the cathedral left a lasting impression on Anna. According to popular belief, the czar had ordered the blinding of the chief architect of the cathedral to prevent him from building another structure that would rival St. Basil's in magnificence. Climbing the narrow spiral staircase, Anna stood for a moment, awe-struck at the detailed floral designs on the pastel walls. On the outside, the splendid onion-like domes glittered in the sunshine, strongly reminding her of the impressive palaces she had seen in the East.

In the evenings, Anna sometimes accompanied her new friends to the Great Imperial Theatre to watch the ballet. She was mesmerized by the gold and crimson interior of the hall and the theatre's colonnade, which featured bronze horses pulling Apollo's chariot. Among the other sights in Moscow, the Imperial Court Museum and the Tretyakov Art Gallery stood out. The former held the regalia of the czars, including ornate carriages, the coat of arms, and cannons on the gilded pedestals. The gallery held paintings of the Russian masters that reinforced Anna's feelings about the importance of cultivating and preserving art in human history. Anna wrote a letter back home in May 1881 in which she promoted the idea that freedom could be expressed through the study of art.

As Anna's travels in Russia were nearing an end, she was excited about her return, knowing that the reading public would eagerly devour the richly detailed articles she had submitted. Besides, Anna had been away from her family for a long time, and she missed her grandchildren, who had recently been writing to her to ask when she would return.

She had also received a letter from Louis, who had returned to Siam once again and was employed at the royal court. His childhood friendship with Prince Chulalongkorn had been renewed and he told Anna that he was happy. This letter sparked a bout of reminiscing as Anna relived her years in Siam. Still, she had mixed feelings about Louis's recent endeavours, but he was a grown man and he had to make his own way in the world. Louis wrote that the prince, now the king of Siam, sent his regards to his old governess. Anna fondly remembered him in her reply to Louis.

By the time Anna returned from Russia, the editors of *The Youth's Companion*, her loyal readers, and her avid fans were ecstatic. She knew she had come back triumphant, and she quickly forgot the discomforts of her journey. Whenever she was asked to speak about her Russian tour, the details and her personal reminiscences electrified the audience. Her articles on her Russian jaunt further cemented her popularity and her reputation as a writer and speaker, and the homecoming lecture she gave in Halifax's Church of England Institute was a resounding success. Long before the lecture, people had started to arrive at the institute, eager to hear about her experiences of travelling alone in a foreign land. Haligonians celebrated the fact that such a brave and famous woman had made her home in their city. Anna told her audience about how difficult life was for Russian women, especially for peasants. At least some of the urban women, she pointed out, had the opportunity to better their circumstances.

Anna, probably without even realizing it, was about to enter another critical phase in her life.

Chapter 5
Anna's Legacy

Anna was instrumental in pushing for social reform for women in Halifax. With her renewed public image, she embarked on meetings and dialogue with the influential members of Halifax society. One of her good friends, Dr. Maria Angwin, had recently become the first female doctor in Halifax. She and Anna met on a regular basis, and Maria often told Anna harrowing tales of the disturbing incidents of injustice she had to face in her line of work. And in the drawing rooms of the wealthy ladies of Halifax, Dr. Angwin spoke with rough compassion about the lives of the female prisoners at the infamous Rockhead Prison. Away from the genteel parties and upper-class manners of Victorian Halifax, there existed a totally different life for those not so privileged. Drinking, fighting, and prostitution were the common afflictions of the city. Perhaps it was not so surprising, thought Anna, given that Halifax was a military garrison.

Prisons were often filled to capacity, and repeat offenders got the worst possible treatment. The mid-nineteenth century saw the prison as a way to keep order in the desperate lives of social outcasts. The idea that prisoners could be reformed to lead wholesome lives and integrate seamlessly into the larger community was still many years away. Rockhead Prison housed not only criminals, but also men and women who lived on the streets. Built to accommodate about 120 inmates, the prisoners often found themselves sharing space with many more than that. The poorhouses were seriously overcrowded; there was no place other than Rockhead for the overflow of paupers.

Dr. Angwin claimed that the prisoners suffered from deadly diseases, the very names of which sent shivers down everyone's spine. Tuberculosis, diphtheria, and typhoid were common visitors to the dark and dingy cells in which the women were lodged. Their main enemy was drink, which wrested away whatever little good sense they may have possessed. Anna heard their stories with great sorrow and compassion and frequently thought back to the wretched garrison life she had lived in as a child in the East. Of course, she never spoke to anyone about that period of her life, not even her family, but the memories and the spectre of hopelessness were always with her.

Anna had been working on her third book during this period and, no doubt, the process resulted in continuing flashbacks from her childhood. *Life and Travel in India* was eventually published in 1884. A few years later, a pivotal event took place in Halifax — a visit from the wife of the governor general of Canada, Ishbel Marjoribanks Gordon, who was the marchioness of Aberdeen. Lady Aberdeen had a keen interest in Canadian women's affairs. Anna and the other ladies in her circle were very excited about the event and a number of activities had been planned for Lady Aberdeen's trip. Among them was the inauguration in Halifax of an autonomous branch of the National Council of Women of Canada. At the prestigious function, Anna related an often-told story she had heard in India when she was a child. (This story has been passed down through many generations and is known around the world. It is sometimes referred to as "The Enlightenment of Keesa Gotami." In one of its many interpretations, it is the story of women's awakening in an ancient society.)

> *About 2000 years ago in India, there lived a girl named Keesa in the great city of Totami. Brought up in a poor farmer's family, Keesa was married off at 15 to a farmer in the neighbouring village, as that was the custom in those days. Within a year, the happy couple was blessed with good news. Keesa gave birth to a baby boy and there was great rejoicing. But fate dealt a severe blow to the adoring*

parents of the little boy. One day, he had a strange seizure and died.

Keesa was inconsolable. She railed against the gods and raved and ranted in agony. Her sorrow was so acute that she beat her breast and wept in anguish. At last she approached the wise Buddha, who was meditating under a banyan tree. "Please let me have some medicine to bring him back to life. You can perform miracles I have heard. Please help my little boy," she begged, sobbing at his feet.

The Buddha looked at her with infinite compassion. He said, "Go and bring me a handful of mustard seeds from a house in the village where no death has taken place. Then I can work a miracle."

Keesa wiped her eyes and nodded eagerly. Then she ran all around the village asking for a handful of mustard seed. But everyone shook their heads and said death had indeed visited their homes at some time or the other. Keesa was extremely tired by this time and her whole body ached, but she had no more tears left. The meaning behind her mission gradually began to sink in and slowly she retraced her steps towards her home. There she laid her baby in his eternal home in the earth and walked back to the Buddha.

"I have been foolish, wise one. There is no such house." The Buddha only said, "You have found the mustard seeds. Go and help others who have suffered as you have."

(Taken from notes Anna made about the story and related at the inaugural meeting of the Local Council of Women in August 1894.)

Anna pointed out the parallels between the story of Keesa and the problem facing the emerging women's movement. She emphasized that the commitment to get involved often begins with a personal loss that ultimately transforms itself into the desire to help others. Thus, it takes only one woman to help others — one woman to become the first link in the chain.

The women were excited and very receptive by the time Anna finished her story. Lady Aberdeen suggested that the Local Council of Women in Halifax work in conjunction with the National Council of Women in Canada, which had its headquarters in Toronto. This was particularly important because more than 60 different groups were represented at the women's council in Halifax. Lady Aberdeen urged young ladies and women to come forward and join various committees that would work in tandem. At the end of Lady Aberdeen's speech, the group exploded into applause.

In the following years, the local council, of which Anna

was an active member, went on to do an enormous amount of work to improve living conditions for the disadvantaged women and children of Halifax. The council's numerous activities were driven by their raison d'être — to empower women. Only by encouraging and helping women to take this step forward could the council ensure a better life for the women of Halifax.

The concept of equal rights for women was in its infancy in Halifax. Some property rights were granted to women, but there was still a long way to go. Generally, women were seen as second-class citizens. Their main lot in life was to live in the shadow of their husbands. There was no real difference between the lives of urban and rural women, either. The province's poorer women worked hard at keeping their households together, often supplementing the family income by weaving, keeping boarders, and sewing. And though the rich women in the cities had help for their households and more financial independence, theirs was a gilded cage.

A subject very close to Anna's heart was the moral and physical welfare of children. The council passed a resolution in 1896 that urged the establishment of a school for truant children from all over Nova Scotia. The prevalent idea at the time was that these children could be trained to become useful citizens. Children who were truant had habitually been sentenced to Industrial School or St. Patrick's Home, which were both reformatories intended for criminals. Anna argued that sending a truant child to either of those places did more harm than good. The ladies who supported her pointed out that most of the truant children came from homes where fathers were either absent or abusive. Anna believed that these children should not be labelled as criminals and that special schools were necessary to meet their needs. In her forthright manner, she stated:

> *I think it is simply this ... that no child who is simply a truant from school should be subjected to any influence but the highest, and that he could not possibly find in a mixed reformatory school.*
>
> (from the March 1896 Report of the Second Annual Meeting of the Local Council of Halifax in Association with the National Council of Women of Canada)

In that same year, Anna moved a resolution at the local council that resulted in gigantic strides for the women's movement — she called for representation of women on public school boards and philanthropic institutions. Anna was convinced that women had to have a say in matters pertaining to the education of their sons and daughters. (It is not clear in the records whether or not this motion was passed, however, it was recorded that other council members heartily agreed with it.)

With Anna at the helm, the women's council then

tackled the subject of the female prisoners at Rockhead. Dr. Maria Angwin had raised the issue of separate lodging for female prisoners at the council's annual meeting in 1894, and Anna and another council member later barged into the mayor's office and demanded this separate accommodation. Anna's concern was that the condition of women who lived at the edges of respectable society was growing worse every day. Respectable upper- and middle-class women could easily be persuaded to work for children and the poor, but turned a blind eye to female prisoners. Victorian prudery and snobbishness deemed such conduct inappropriate.

As in the barracks towns of colonial India, the lives of poor women in Halifax offered little chance for improvement. The notorious Barrack Street below the Citadel was referred to as "a nest of brothels and dance houses." The military men were frequent customers at the brothels, and the women's lives continued to be filled with drink, disease, and hopelessness. Crime was a way of life. Albermarle Street, also just outside the Citadel, was a den of iniquity in the eyes of respectable Haligonians. Women of doubtful morality, often drunk and quarrelsome, hung around the street at all hours of the day and night.

Dr. Angwin often had cause to frequent Albermarle Street. At the council meetings, she recounted with horror how young children were often seen late at night, smoking openly on the streets and swearing at passersby. She proposed a curfew, forbidding children under 16 to be out on the streets after 9 p.m., but Anna opposed this resolution on the grounds that it was a blow to civil liberty:

> *I would beg to say that, owing to the condition of things here, we would have to proceed very carefully. It would seem a breach of the Habeas Corpus Act to infringe upon the freedom of our citizens, and hence, in bringing this legislative measure forwarded by the Women's Local Council, we have to be very careful not to get the entire city, in fact the whole province, set against us as being officious and overdoing things.*

> (from the March 1896 Report of the Second Annual Meeting of the Local Council of Halifax in Association with the National Council of Women of Canada)

One of the newspapers of the period, *The Chronicle,* applauded the efforts of Anna and the ladies of the council who attempted, against tremendous odds, to better the conditions of the lower rungs of Halifax society.

Another matter soon came to Anna's attention. Many immigrants from Europe arrived at Halifax's teeming harbour. Female immigrants, particularly if they were in impoverished circumstances, often experienced male harassment and degradation at the immigration centre. Anna advocated the appointment of a female matron at the waterfront immigration shed. At the next council meeting, she moved that a committee be appointed to interview a candidate for the matron's job. The motion was successfully carried, and Anna was placed on the committee.

During her years on the council, the right of women to vote was one of Anna's main concerns. One memorable night at a council meeting she spoke with great conviction about why women should be allowed to vote. Another speaker was the American educator and reformer May Eliza Sewall, a pioneer of the women's movement in the United States. The meeting was packed with spectators, who had undoubtedly been drawn by Sewall's reputation as a firebrand orator. The atmosphere was electric as Anna took centre stage and spoke eloquently of how Canadian women were every bit as committed to the suffragist cause as American women and about the denial of women's entry into most professions. Women were only finding employment as teachers, nurses, or factory workers. They were capable of much more, she exclaimed to wild applause from the crowd. Then Anna advanced a radical opinion — if women were not allowed to vote, she said — they should not have to pay taxes. It was clear that Anna was pointing out to Sewall that Canadian women had already embraced the suffragist cause and were on equal ground with their American counterparts. There was a great burst of cheering at her words and the photographers' bulbs exploded blindingly in the Assembly Chambers.

Among the members of the council, Anna had several enthusiastic supporters for her ideas and vision involving women. Aside from Dr. Angwin, the two Misses Ritchie (professors at Dalhousie University) and Mrs. Kenny were among her close personal friends, and they fought many battles together. Edith Archibald was another friend who remembered Anna as being a fearless crusader who was never afraid to speak her mind.

Anna also served for several years as president of the Halifax Women's Suffrage Association and was always an active and vocal representative for the group. The suffragist question, however, was not to be resolved in those early years. Much of the fault lay with women themselves, many of whom considered politics an unfeminine pursuit that interfered with their God-given duties. And, often, those in high places supported them. The attorney general, the Honourable J.W. Longley, believed that a woman's place was at home. Anna was absolutely livid with rage when she first heard Longley's publicly proffered views on suffrage. Many years later, as suffragists like Anna continued to agitate for fair recognition of women, a bill was introduced in the legislature to give voting rights to women. Attorney General Longley was instrumental in blocking the passage of this bill, and the Catholic Church's opposition to female suffrage added fuel to the fire. It was long after Anna's time, not until 1918, that Nova Scotia's women won the right to vote. But if it had not been for the spirited struggle of Anna and other suffragists in the province, the process would have taken much longer.

By this time, Anna was also heavily involved in setting up the Victorian Order of Nurses, various women's art associations, and the National Home Reading Union, organizations that worked with the local women's council to better conditions for women.

In 1887, Queen Victoria's Golden Jubilee celebrations were animating all of Halifax, and people could talk of nothing else. Haligonians were agog with excitement, and a great function was being planned to mark the occasion. Anna was deeply involved with the numerous committees that were hosting events to mark the occasion. However, she had the foresight to focus on a goal of her own — to create something permanent that would stay in the city — and be remembered long after the celebrations ended. The ceremonies surrounding the festivities, she believed, were merely transient in nature, and people would remember them only until the next big event. There had to be something more important than the individual events themselves — something that would cement the Golden Jubilee celebrations, but would also leave a legacy for the people of Nova Scotia.

For many days Anna thought about her idea. Then, late one night when she could not sleep and was mulling over the situation, her eye fell on a print by the Russian master Ivan Shishkin, called *The Corn*. She sighed with pleasure as the painting brought back vivid memories of the Russian landscape. Her thoughts drifted to how art has the capacity to transport a person into a realm of delight. As she recalled standing on the steps of the Tretyakov Art Gallery in Moscow ,she wished that there were an institute in Halifax that encouraged the study of art. It took her very little time to figure out that she had just found the project she was looking for. The concept of an art school took root in Anna's mind. At the time, there was no institution in the city that taught technical illustration and drawing. Many students had to leave the province to pursue their vocations. Anna was convinced that such an institution would be an incredible asset to her city. In addition, an art institute would become a permanent part of Halifax and of Nova Scotia, and an exciting way of commemorating the queen's jubilee.

The art community was already thriving in Halifax by the late 1800s. The Halifax Chess, Pencil, and Brush Club, which had been formed 100 years before, had enjoyed a good run among artistically inclined citizens. Private lessons with well-known artists were available, as well. As early as 1809, an advertisement for lessons with the portrait painter and miniaturist John Thomson had appeared in the Halifax daily newspaper, and the notable artist William Gush had set up a school in the city to give instruction in landscape and marine painting. Dalhousie University, which was established in 1818, had a few artists working as teachers. Acadia University, in Wolfville, also offered drawing and painting classes. In addition, around 1831, the Halifax Mechanics Institute had begun to offer courses in the fine arts, which included drawing, art history, and architecture. By the 1860s, there were the first stirrings to set up an institution devoted to an education in the fine arts.

The city already had an expectant look about it. Plans were being drawn up for jubilee celebrations in the elegant drawing rooms of society matrons. Amid tinkling china and excited conversation, notes were hastily written and acted upon. Committees were formed, alliances cemented, and a vision created — all with the objective of glorifying Queen Victoria with a memorable tribute. Halifax, Canada's fourth largest city at the time with a population of 35,000, felt compelled to show how much Haligonians revered the queen and all she stood for. The Mi'kmaq were prominently featured in the celebrations and the province's St. John's Ambulance Association was scheduled to perform its first public service at the pageant. Floats, gardens, and commemorative buildings were all a part of the plan. Gentlemen in waistcoats and wigs went about their assigned duties with fervour; ladies in their silk dresses wore ostrich-feather hats and spoke in hushed voices about the torchlight processions, exciting sporting events, and mock battles.

Throughout the jubilee celebrations, Anna continued to pursue her dream of an art institute. Her concept of an institution for vocational training in the mechanical arts demonstrated once more her unusual foresight and vision. Anna had been referred to as an "eloquent advocate of the value of education in the fine and industrial arts." As always, once she made up her mind about a direction, she immediately went into high gear. She explained to her friends that not everybody could paint like Monet, but by having access to great works of art, they would surely learn to appreciate art and enjoy its aesthetic pleasures. There was also, she pointed out, an obvious economic benefit for Halifax that would result from the enterprise. Anna's friends were, at first, a little skeptical. They reminded her that there were already small local schools that gave training in the decorative arts. Anna hastened to clear up any confusion. In her elaborations of the potential of such an institution, she made it clear that she did not want it to be merely a school for ladies engaged in the gentle pursuits of watercolours and oil painting. She intended it mainly for labourers, draftsmen, and tradesmen who were in no position to develop and hone their skills in Halifax. Anna emphasized that no school in Nova Scotia offered this kind of training, and that going elsewhere, to the United States or Europe to study, was hopelessly fanciful for many people.

Anna knew that she had to recruit the ladies of the women's council to see her idea to fruition. In order to convince the council, Anna circulated an article she had written earlier, "The Art Movement in America" for *Century Magazine*. The article suggested establishing art schools to create interest in the mechanical and industrial arts. Because of her extensive travels, Anna knew that art schools, museums, and exhibitions pumped life into a city. She declared to her influential friends that Halifax had been ready for its own art school for some time. With that possibility foremost in her mind, and with the enthusiastic support of her friends, Anna became the vice president of the original board of directors of the school-to-be. Her dear friend, Mrs. Jeremiah Kenny, the wife of a leading insurance broker in the city, was always at her side thinking up ways to raise funds for the school. Anna cashed in on her abilities and name and gave lectures all over the country to raise money, but this was not the only trump card she had up her sleeve.

Anna had another brilliant idea — an art-on-loan exhibition where interesting artifacts and curios could be displayed. It was a resounding success and raised an unheard of sum in those days — $5,000. Over 10,000 people attended. One of the exhibits was two palm-leaf manuscripts containing passages of the *Rig Veda* (the Hindu scriptures), on loan from Anna's personal collection. Other Oriental exhibits of Anna's drew wondering gasps and murmurs of admiration. As well, fine laces, original and copied works of the Old Masters, and Burmese idols were displayed. Local artists were also represented at the exhibition. George Harvey, Florence Sealy, and Frances Jones Bannerman showed their works, which were much appreciated by art-loving Haligonians.

Finally, the Victoria School of Art and Design came to life on October 31, 1887. Its purpose was to provide "technical instruction and art culture" to the people who needed it as part of their jobs. One of the institute's key objectives

— long promoted by Anna and the council — was to open a new avenue of income for women. Once the money was procured, classes started at the Victoria School of Art and Design, which was first housed on the upper floors of the Union Bank building at the intersection of Hollis and Prince Streets. Anna had convinced her son-in-law Thomas to arrange for the rental of the premises. In the first year, the school's rent was $350, excluding taxes, and its enrollment was 125 students. Daytime classes consisted primarily of women who sought to be drawing teachers. Anna also organized a Saturday morning children's art instruction class, attended by 19 neatly dressed girls and boys who brought their pencils and drawing boards to study freehand drawing and elementary design. The aim was to prepare budding artists to become future art scholars, and the expectation was that they would enrol at the school when they neared adulthood. Before long, Anna was able to pass along to the women's council favourable reports from factory workers, machinists, architects, and technical hands about their studies at the Victoria School of Art and Design.

Among the staff of the new art and design school was George Harvey, the headmaster for freehand drawing, design, illustration, clay modelling, and painting in oil and water. An engineer, J.T. Larkin, who taught geometrical and mechanical drawing, designing, and planning, supported him. Miss. Evans, an honours graduate from the Pennsylvania Museum of Industrial and Technical Art, also began to teach classes. Her vast experience and lively imagination proved a boon for students.

The province of Nova Scotia and the city of Halifax provided much of the financial assistance. The House of Assembly promised an $800 annual grant to the school and agreed to donate the Assembly Chamber at Province House for an exhibition Anna organized. Katherine N. Evans and Elizabeth S. Nutt, prominent activists in Halifax who supported the school and lent enormous prestige and goodwill to the cause, assisted Anna in her efforts for the school.

The Victoria School of Art and Design and the Halifax Ladies College soon became the two most famous educational institutions in the Halifax area. Under the stewardship of Headmaster Harvey, free classes in drawing, clay modelling, and object drawing were offered to interested students from the Halifax Ladies College. The school of art and design rapidly came to be viewed as an important force for the economic development of the province. All over Nova Scotia there was a growing demand for artists and skilled draftsmen, and many graduates from the Victoria School of Art and Design found rewarding employment.

At this point, Anna embarked on another adventure that had unforeseen repercussions for the then thriving school of art and design. The school was running smoothly and Anna was in dire need of an extended break. She told Avis and Thomas that she would take her granddaughter Ann with her on a tour to Europe. Ann Fyshe was a student at the Halifax Ladies' College and was also taking special lessons from the Conservatory of Music. The family was living in the Sunnyside district, at the corner of Dutch Village and Mumford Roads, at the time. Anna was firmly convinced that Ann, who was a gifted pianist, needed the experienced guidance of a more talented teacher of music. Naturally, young Ann jumped at the chance.

In the end, the family decided that Anna and Ann, as well as Avis and all the other grandchildren, would take the trip together. The cost of this sojourn was not a hardship as Thomas was in a well-paid position with the bank and Anna was independently wealthy. Thus, in early 1888, Anna and her brood sailed away from the Halifax Harbour for a five-year educational trip to Europe. Only Thomas Fyshe stayed behind, to reside alone at the city's Waverly Hotel, which was situated in downtown Halifax. When Anna left Halifax with her family, she had a definite plan in mind. Young Ann was a serious pianist, and her dedication to music made her grandmother very proud. One of Anna's primary goals in life had been the education and upbringing of her many grandchildren, including Louis's child, Anna Harriet, who had lived with them for some time. Grandmother Anna ruled over her offspring with an iron hand and was very conscious of feeding their young minds with sound ideas. Anna's grandchildren were quite used to their grandmother wielding enormous influence over them, and it was Anna they looked to for guidance, not their mother. Deciding to take Ann and the others on this extensive tour was not just a whim. Anna herself enrolled in a Sanskrit course at the University of Leipzig, where she hoped to brush up on her skills in the ancient language, as well as act as chaperone for the children.

While they were away, Anna corresponded regularly with friends who were involved with the Victoria School of Art and Design. Unfortunately, Anna's five-year absence had resulted in considerable administrative problems for the school, which was still in its infancy when Anna left for Europe and in need of a steady hand and fixed goal setting to guide it. Many a storm had come its way, and the school directors had often wished that Anna were there to take the reins in her capable hands. In addition, the popularity of the art and design school with the community had been overestimated, and the board of directors soon found they were short of money. Collecting the school's fees proved to be vexing, and pledges were not being renewed. It was not that people did not want to pay fees. It was simply that there was no concerted effort by the school administrators to manage fee collection effectively. The lackadaisical approach to collecting overdue fees was killing the school, and the lack of ongoing fundraising had made the public complacent.

When her ship finally docked at the Halifax Harbour five years later, Anna was completely immersed in her family and more than satisfied with the trip. She knew that their European sojourn had given the family a much-needed boost of culture and excitement. Now she was prepared to pick up the thread of her life in Halifax again. One of Anna's first thoughts was to find out how bad things were at the art school but she delayed doing this until, with customary thoroughness, she settled her family in at 235 Pleasant Street, an elegant downtown building.

As soon as things were settled at home, Anna paid a visit to the Victoria School of Art and Design. In the meantime, her friends had visited her to apprise her of the situation. Before long, Anna was presiding over the meeting of the board of directors and looking over the papers with a frown. As she glanced over the financial statements and listened to the reports of the other directors and board members, Anna's displeasure was obvious, so she did what she was best at and took charge. By the time her first meeting was over, she had appointed a committee to seek additional funds, set up a new attendance and fees register designed to be maintained without fail, and made sure that all the teachers knew and followed the rules.

There were murmurs that day, some in admiration and some in resentment, about her attitude, but Anna knew that she had to take control in order to save her dream from going down the drain. She took a good look at the administrative structure of the school and discussed the situation with Avis and Thomas to determine the best course of action. Since the school was primarily her idea, Anna was able to step in and take over stewardship as one of the directors, despite the five-year gap created by her absence.

In the succeeding years, Ozias Dodge and Charles

Waterbury replaced Headmaster George Harvey, but neither lasted. So, why not have a woman manage the school?
Obviously, it would have to be someone capable of taking on
the responsibility and willing to face opposition. At the next
board meeting, Anna courageously faced uproar when she
voiced this view. Despite considerable resistance and much
grumbling, Anna prevailed and the Victoria School of Art
and Design appointed its first female head, Katherine Evans.
Though she came highly recommended by Anna, there were
a few negative-minded skeptics who felt that a woman would
be incapable of tackling the administrative responsibilities of
such an institution. But Anna ignored the naysayers, as she
enthusiastically and confidently handed over the reins of the
school to Evans.

Under Evans' tenure, the school revived. At a meeting of the Local Council of Women in 1896, Anna reiterated
that it was "the duty of legislators and teachers" to ensure
that an ongoing supply of trained artists and educators be
available in Halifax. She urged the council to find a way to
give the school a permanent home. The province's premier,
William Stevens Fielding, promised to attend to the matter
of a permanent site for the Victoria School of Art and Design,
but nothing concrete emerged and, over the years, the school
was relocated many times to accommodate more students,
more equipment, and new rental leases.

In 1909, the school relocated from the Union Bank
building to the Old National School overlooking Grande

Parade Square on Argyle Street. In 1925, 10 years after Anna Leonowens died, the school was incorporated and became the Nova Scotia College of Art. In 1957, it moved to a church on Coburg Road. Finally, in 1978, it began occupation of its present campus in downtown Halifax. By then it had become a degree-granting university. It is now called the Nova Scotia College of Art and Design (NSCAD) and students from all over the world come to take instruction in its various disciplines.

Chapter 6
Montreal and Anna's Final Years

fter years of fighting for the now world famous school of art and design, Anna's life took a different turn.

In 1899, Thomas was offered a prestigious position at the bank in Montreal and the entire family decided to move on. At first, Anna had toyed with the idea of staying in Halifax, but when she told her family, there were immediate outbursts of anguish. Avis, especially, would not even consider the idea of her mother staying behind, and she, Thomas, and the grandchildren begged her not to abandon them. At this stage in Anna's life, family was paramount, so she put all thoughts of independent living out of her head and made preparations to leave her beloved Halifax.

Leaving Halifax had been harder than she thought. The

art school, which still needed her fighting spirit, was there and she had cultivated a large number of friends in the city. The farewell Anna received from Halifax was warm and sincere. Her friends recounted how much she had done for the city and people from many walks of life came to see her and thank her for her involvement in the life of ordinary people. She was feted at many functions, and newspapers described her contribution to the city and the art school. But by the time all goodbyes had been said, Anna was content and ready for a new experience.

Excitement stirred in Anna's heart as she arrived in Montreal. As her eyes wandered over the broad outline of the St. Lawrence River, the beauty of the quayside struck her. Montreal was a thriving commercial city whose builders and merchants had made their fortunes through furs, logging, and commerce. There was a hard glitter to life in Montreal. Anna's family lived first on Sherbrooke Street, and then on McTavish Street with McGill University campus but a stone's throw away. Anna soon made friends, and her new acquaintances told her stories about Montreal and its many famous visitors, who were drawn, over the years, by its charming combination of history and wealth. Coincidentally, one was the great reformer and activist, the Reverend Henry Ward Beecher, the brother of Harriet Beecher Stowe. Anna was delighted to hear that this commanding, dignified, and genial man had given a speech at the Jacques Cartier Pier in Montreal 20 years earlier. Apparently, the echoes of his speech had filtered across the entire country and the fervour of his words still moved many. Reverend Beecher had told the crowds that no one had the right to strip another human being of dignity. These were Anna's thoughts exactly — and she excitedly told her new friends how she had been influenced by the reverend's work, in addition to that of his sister.

One of Anna's greatest pleasures in Montreal was to spend her evenings with her grandchildren at the Victoria Skating Rink, one of the biggest indoor rinks on the continent at the time. The ice covered 929 square metres and the skating rink had an impressive promenade platform. Light from the 500 gas jets filtered through the coloured globes of glass, making the rink seem like a fairyland. Anna often sat in the spectators' gallery and watched the young people, including her grandchildren, glide over the ice, skating to waltzes and mazurkas. Her enjoyment was always intense, even though the cold air hurt her lungs in her advancing years (she was 78 years old at the time).

These wholesome and joyous activities were, however, only one part of the city's life. As in Halifax, there was a seedy side to Montreal, made up of less fortunate people who fought disease and relentless poverty. Even at the skating rink, Anna never allowed herself to forget the degradation and utter hopelessness of poor women and their children. In big cities everywhere, industry had provided additional jobs for women, but in its wake had created unsafe and unsanitary conditions. Disease rampaged through the neighbourhood of Griffintown, which was notorious in Montreal for its filth, sickness, and poverty. Just like Barrack and Albermarle Streets in Halifax, Griffintown spawned hideous diseases like typhoid and diphtheria. Anna despaired at these conditions and tried to help the hapless inhabitants as much as she could, but age was slowing her down, and she no longer had the energy she had in Halifax.

Still, she never gave up. One project that engaged her attention was the Baby and Foundling Hospital. There were allegations of baby farming, a common practice at the time, whereby orphans were given to foster families in exchange for a sizeable amount of money for their care. Many a time, it was noted, these orphans died suddenly and mysteriously, and the foster families failed to return the money. Anna could not bear it that such a practice was allowed to flourish, and she campaigned vigorously among the clergy and the hospital authorities for an end to it.

On another level, Anna's fame as a lecturer on the Orient continued to grow, and she was invited to lecture at McGill University, where she frequently regaled students with her stories. Furthermore, young and old alike often came by the family home in the chilly evenings to discuss various topics with her.

Anna also taught classes in Sanskrit at McGill. Her love of Oriental languages was still strong, and she always had interesting anecdotes to tell her students. One was about her Sanskrit teacher at the University of Leipzig (during her five-year educational sojourn), who at first refused to let her attend his classes because she was a woman. She explained that in the typically male-dominated sphere of academia in Victorian times, he probably could not imagine a sharp intellect in a woman. Nevertheless, she eventually convinced him to take her on as a student and he quickly discovered, perhaps to his chagrin, that she had a remarkable affinity for the language, culture, and customs of the East.

One of Anna's favourite places in Montreal was the Redpath Museum and Library, which was located across from her home. Surrounded by the dark wooden panelling of the library, in front of the ornate fireplace, Anna spent many delightful hours scanning the ancient texts. Then, one day, an invitation to lecture on Egyptian antiquities arrived in the mail. It was an opportunity to reflect on her past experiences, and she fondly recalled her time with Reverend Badger and their tour of the Middle East and Egypt. While on this first trip when she was in her mid-teens, Anna had written an account of her journey. Reviewing the Redpath Museum's Egyptian collection, she felt herself going back in time, soaking up the wonders of ancient Egypt. Among the hieroglyphic texts, the showy amulets, and unusual ornaments, Anna jotted down notes for her lecture. With remembered pleasure, her eyes alighted on the Redpath Museum's prize exhibits, the mummies and bronze figures of Egypt. In her mind's eye, she saw the crowded *souks* with merchants spreading out their exquisite handmade rugs. She heard the din and bustle of horse-drawn carriages, and the morning invitation to prayer that issued from the domed mosques.

Never far from her mind was the thought that by adding these striking touches to her lectures and writings, she was making them more believable and more interesting for her North American audiences. Since she had been to these places, she was able to bring an unmatched touch of truth to her lectures. Her talk on Egyptian artifacts was a resounding success, and her Redpath Museum audience went home that frosty Montreal night thinking about that great ancient civilization.

But Anna's idyllic life was about to come to an end. Life had been full and rewarding for the family in Montreal for those first three years. Then, suddenly, a tragic incident occurred that permanently affected the entire family and came very close to destroying Anna's health and breaking her spirit. In the spring of 1902, Avis decided to accompany her husband on a business trip to Toronto. By this time, Thomas was a well-known banker and a prominent member of Montreal society. He was frequently away from home on trips and, though Avis usually stayed home, this time she decided to accompany him. Anna, a little reluctantly, of course, bid a fond and unconcerned goodbye to Avis.

A short time after the couple departed, Anna received news that Avis had suddenly fallen ill with food poisoning. Next came the crushing announcement that Avis had died. Anna reeled from the shock and was plunged into a black void of grief and depression. Thomas was also devastated. His only way of dealing with this new life was to throw himself relentlessly into his work. It was extremely hard on Anna, but now with eight children who had just lost their mother under her care, there was little time or opportunity to worry about her own needs.

Anna quickly found she had no time to wallow in grief. She knew the family would fall apart if she were not strong; but the thought that she had outlived three children was more than she could bear: she'd outlived her beloved Avis and, many years ago, the two infants in India. On top of this, she had known for years that she had lost her son Louis as well, albeit in another way, and it was as bitter as gall to her. At least she still had her grandchildren, who looked to her for support in this time of deep sorrow. Slowly, over time, the children learned to look back on Avis's sudden departure from their lives with a little less pain. And Anna gradually learned to accept what fate had dealt her. But she was tormented in her dreams by snapshots of Avis as a child, as a young girl, and then as a mature wife and mother. Throughout their lives, with every passing year, Anna and her daughter had grown closer. Eventually, Anna began to look back on those early days with fondness rather than tears.

James, Max, Anna, Avis, and their cousin Anna Harriet were all students at McGill University. They did very well academically and frequently brought home accolades and awards. Anna cherished these, and when she was nearing the end of her time on this earth, her greatest pleasures were the accomplishments of her grandchildren.

As she aged, Anna became more reflective ... how many worlds she had passed through ... how many experiences she had had! Despite the onset of old age though, Anna had found it difficult to give up her zeal for community work, but after Avis's death, even giving a lecture required an almost insurmountable effort. However, the Fyshe household continued to hold "open house" days for Anna's admirers, who still wanted to hear all about her adventures and get her autograph.

Eastern philosophy, be it Hinduism or Buddhism, had attracted Anna ever since childhood. She never considered herself as belonging to or practicing a particular religion. Ever since the first time she had heard the epic stories of India's mythic Hindu heroes, she had been under their spell. The old monk who taught her the Siamese language in Bangkok gave her a solid grounding in the Buddha's teachings. Now, in the autumn of her life, Anna found herself drawn to these ancient teachings because they appealed to her common sense and satisfied her deep longing for inner spirituality. Anna had begun to sense that her work on this earth was done, that the wheel would stop spinning soon. The feeling of an impending end compelled her to ponder on the after-life and the concepts of reincarnation, karma, and justice. She was constantly comforted by the belief that beyond lay a reunion with her beloved Avis.

Montreal and Anna's Final Years

In 1914, World War I broke out. A catastrophic series of events began to unfold, and the resulting chaos echoed throughout the world. Europe rang with cries of victory and defeat. In Canada, young men only 18 and 19 years old were suddenly drafted into military service. They were raring to go so they could become men and heroes. People spent their days listening feverishly to radio broadcasts. Mothers fainted and wives wept in despair as Canada's brave troops poured from the landing crafts onto the beaches in Europe.

Anna, in her last days, wondered if the world had gone mad. Everything suddenly seemed to be disintegrating. In the room where she lay, only half-conscious, pictures of her childhood floated through her mind. She remembered running up the fort ramparts in Poona, saw her sister Eliza's face, and mourned her two dead babies. She thought about the voyages, the oceans, and the boundaries she had crossed. Death was just one more boundary. On January 19, 1915, Anna Leonowens died at the age of 84.

Epilogue

The story of Anna Leonowens life was revived some time after her death. There was and still is a magic about her life story that will endure over time. It wasn't really the books she wrote that precipitated this revival. The books might have languished away in libraries for years, her memory alive only in her descendants — if it hadn't been for Margaret Landon's book — and Hollywood.

It all started with the publication of *Anna and the King of Siam*, written by a woman who was fascinated by Anna's life and times. Margaret Landon had lived in Siam as a missionary between 1926 and 1937. She often spent her leisure time roaming the streets of Trang and visiting Bangkok. Slowly, the ancient history of Siam began to seep into her consciousness. It was during her sojourn there that she first heard about Anna Leonowens. When she returned to the United States she wrote her book, which was based on research she had done while in Siam and the material in two of Anna's four books. Landon's *Anna and the King of Siam* became a huge success. Reviewers of the time called it "an intriguing, historical tale based on ancient Siamese records and the secret diaries, letters, and conversations of Anna in Bangkok that reads like fiction but is amazingly genuine."

Today's reader may find the book dull, heavy-handed

with its Christian versus pagan theme, and its attempt to exoticize Thailand, as Siam came to be called in 1939. Nevertheless, Landon's book served as a launching pad for the resurrection of the life of Anna Leonowens. Barely a decade later, in 1946, 20th Century Fox made a movie entitled *Anna and the King of Siam*, based on Landon's book. It starred Rex Harrison as the king of Siam and Irene Dunn as Anna. The film was an Oscar-winning hit. It depicted Anna as a strong-willed nineteenth century British governess, who was engaged in a battle of wits with an equally forceful Siamese monarch.

Inspired by the success of this movie, 20th Century Fox decided on a remake of the movie in 1956. This time it was a musical entitled *The King and I*. Yul Brynner portrayed King Mongkut, and Deborah Kerr played the role of Anna. This version of the film also won several Oscars. Broadway versions have often been performed and the gorgeous scenes, magnificent stage settings, exotic costumes, and excellent music never fail to captivate audiences.

Toward the end of the century there was renewed interest in Anna's story. In 1999, Warner Brothers produced an animated version of *The King and I*. Directed by Richard Rich, the movie more or less adheres to the highly fictionalized portrait of Anna as the crusader who brought Western ideas of fair play and civilization to pagan Siam. The story of Tuptim (a complete fabrication, according to historians) is included in the movie. Both children and adults seem to think it is fitting that there is a suggestion of romance between the king and Anna.

In that same year, 20th Century Fox brought out yet another movie, this time called *Anna and the King*, which starred Jodie Foster as Anna, and Chow Yun-Fat as the king. According to the publicity release:

> Anna and the King *is an epic tale set in Thailand in the late nineteenth century and chronicles the true life adventures of British governess Anna Leonowens, who is hired by the king of Siam to educate his 58 children. The story is based on historical information and Leonowens' published works.*

Directed by Andy Tennant, Jodie Foster portrays a prim and proper British Victorian determined not to be cowed by the arrogant king. The film is a representation of Anna's life, but there is more fantasy than fact in it. Battles with the Burmese, elephant treks, and swinging bridges in the lush forests of Thailand make for great visuals. However, some of the movie is difficult to believe, such as a scene in which Anna teaches the king how to eat with a knife and fork. (The film, incidentally, was actually shot in Malaysia.)

The reaction of the Thai people towards the depiction of their revered king makes interesting reading. Both *The King and I* and *Anna and the King* were banned in Thailand.

Epilogue

This is hardly surprising because the Thais respect their history and their monarchy and consider the character of King Mongkut, as shown in the movie version, to be fatuous and ridiculous. In reality, the king was an enlightened monarch who spent more than 20 years studying to be a monk. He was well versed in traditional culture and in the Buddhist scriptures. As well, he was familiar with several languages, namely Sanskrit, Pali, Latin, French, and English. One of his keen interests was modern administration practice. He also studied astronomy, gadgetry, and shipbuilding. The Thais believe that the depiction of King Mongkut in the American movie versions as a "noble savage" is derogatory. The battle between fact and fiction still rages.

What would Anna have made of all this? The no-nonsense yet feminine do-gooder from the movies does not mesh with Anna's real personality. In Anna's writings there was never even the slightest suggestion of a romantic involvement with King Mongkut. Knowing the life story of this ardent feminist, one gets the feeling that Anna would hardly have approved.

Anna Leonowens's attitude towards the Thais was not a simplified question of "good versus evil" or a taming of a "savage race" to enlighten the natives into acceptance of a "civilized" Western or Christian perspective of life. Anna genuinely loved the Thai people and had a deep-seated understanding of the king's psyche.

Let us hope that one day, a director or playwright will

give us the real Anna Leonowens in a memorable film that will capture her true character for future generations.

Anna wrote four books in her lifetime, which were more historical fiction than history. Soon after her first book, *The English Governess in the Siamese Court: Recollections of Six Years at the Royal Palace at Bangkok* (1870) came out, Anna became a celebrity and North America's reading public was curious to know more about her. These were Victorian times and Anna had created an air of mystery around her life. Who was this woman? Where had she come from? Shrewdly, Anna managed to capture some of the ideals and sensibilities of the day in her writing. Her first book spoke eloquently of her horror at the moral degradation of slaves in Siam, and her revulsion regarding the injustices that occurred in the royal household. Her second book, *The Romance of the Harem* (1872), was also highly successful, and this time Anna was a well-known and sought-after speaker.

In 1884, while Anna was still living in Halifax, her third book, *Life and Travel in India: Being Recollections of a Journey Before the Days of the Railroads* was published, but it was not as well received as her first two. Five years after that, she published her fourth and final book, *Our Asiatic Cousins* (1889), which, again, was not very popular with the reading public. Was Anna losing her touch? Only her first two books really made a dramatic impact. Does it matter? And if she is accused of embellishing the tales in her writing, surely it is a minor fault.

Epilogue

It may have been that Anna Leonowens was simply running out of new material. Experienced and successful writers know it is important to seek new subjects and material, but Anna's writing was always secondary to her lifelong commitment of working towards a more fair and just world. She was an educated and experienced traveller in a time when women lived in a circumscribed world. Throughout her entire life, Anna focused her energy and attention on realms far beyond her writing. She is widely acclaimed as a feminist, as a strong supporter of the women's suffrage movement, and as the founder of a world-famous art school that exists to this day.

In the end, Anna remains one of the most fascinating characters of Victorian Canada. The veil she drew over her early life has shifted only slightly. Facets of her character — complex, yet startling in its simplicity — continue to cause interest and debate. Anna's was not an easy life. Her remarkable journey holds a lesson for all of us, her latter-day admirers. There is much we can learn from her even though she stands separated from us by a gulf of almost a century. Her genuine interest in the welfare of women and children, her passion for the arts, and her sheer determination in bringing up her family single-handed are qualities that cannot fail to excite admiration.

Two of the Canadian cities she lived in, Halifax and Montreal, were changed indelibly by the unique mark she put on them. The energy for which she was famous charged and electrified the communities in which she lived. In Montreal, she served as president of the Baby and Foundling Hospital for some years, despite her advanced age and failing health. Earlier, in Halifax, she agitated for better conditions for female prisoners at a time when they were largely ignored by society. Her revolutionary ideas about suffrage and women's rights have earned her a permanent place in Canada's history. It is interesting to note that, despite her well-publicized anti-slavery stance, there is some debate about how much Anna really did for the considerable black population in Halifax. Though Anna Leonowens was progressive and broad in her outlook, it seems she could never fully overcome the racist barriers of her background and upbringing. Even in her books and writings, where she mentions Harriet Beecher Stowe's famous book *Uncle Tom's Cabin*, Anna largely ignores the real race issues.

And if she has been condemned by some as a falsifier, perhaps we can look the other way at her literary misdemeanours. She was a single mother who had the sole responsibility for her young children. If people wanted sensational tales from the Siamese harem, "Let them have them," she might well have said.

Anna died on January 19, 1915. She is buried in Montreal's Mount Royal Cemetery, joined in eternal rest with her gentle daughter, Avis. On her tombstone are the words —

Epilogue

ANNA LEONOWENS
1831 – 1915
Duty was the guide of her life and the love of her heart.
To her, life was beautiful and good.
She was a benediction to all who knew her
and a breath of the spirit of God.

Further Reading

Borrett Coates, William. *Historic Halifax*. Toronto, Ontario: Ryerson Press, 1948.

Bruce, Harry. *An Illustrated History of Nova Scotia*. Halifax, Nova Scotia: Nimbus, 1997.

Choyce, Leslie. *Nova Scotia – Shaped by the Sea: A Living History*. New York: Nimbus, 1996.

Collard, Edgar Andrew. *Montreal Yesterdays*. Toronto: Ontario: Longmans Canada, 1963.

Kaplan, Robert D. *Eastward to Tartary – Travels in the Balkans, the Middle East and the Caucasus*. New York: Random House, 2000.

Keay, Julia. *With Passport and Parasol – The Adventures of Seven Victorian Ladies*. London: BBC Books, 1989.

Landon, Margaret. *Anna and the King of Siam*. The John Day Company, 1944.

Further Reading

Leonowens, Anna. *The English Governess at the Siamese Court: Recollections of Six Years at the Royal Palace at Bangkok.* London, England: Trubner and Co. 1870.

Leonowens, Anna. *The Romance of the Harem.* Philadelphia, USA: Porter & Coates, 1873.

Leonowens, Anna. *Life and Travel in India: Being Recollections of a Journey Before the Days of Railroads.* London, England: Porter & Coates, 1884.

Leonowens, Anna. *Our Asiatic Cousins.* Boston, USA: D. Lothrop & Co., 1889.

Middleton, Dorothy. *Victorian Lady Travellers.* London: Routledge & Kegan Paul, 1965.

Raddall, Thomas H. *Halifax Warden of the North.* Halifax, Nova Scotia: Nimbus, 1993.

Smith Dow, Leslie. *Anna Leonowens: Life After The King and I.* Halifax, Nova Scotia: Pottersfield, 1998.

Acknowledgments

I have been an admirer of Anna Leonowens for a long time. In the true feminist tradition, she shattered many of the myths surrounding women at the time, in particular that they should always be "nice" and "polite" and that they could never rise without the help of a man.

This book is my interpretation of how Anna's life shaped up. I am indebted to the excellent work on Anna Leonowens's life by Leslie Smith Dow, author of *Anna Leonowens: Life After The King and I*. Most of my book is a representation of Anna's fascinating life, her origins, and the road she travelled.

A number of people helped shape this book: Chantelle Taylor, reference librarian at the Halifax Public Library (Spring Garden Road); Virginia Clark, researcher at Halifax's Public Archives; Harold Pearse for his valuable suggestions about sources of information; and Janice Fralic–Brown of the NSCAD University Library, for her help when I was at the NSCAD.

Heartfelt thanks to my editor, Dianne Smyth, for her skills, and to Joyce Glasner, Jill Foran, and Kara Turner at Altitude Publishing for their faith in my abilities.

Also, deep gratitude and love to my husband and daughters, who never let me doubt that this book would happen.

About the Author

Moushumi Chakrabarty grew up in Poona, India, and now makes her home in Mississauga, Ontario, as well as on the Internet. She has been writing for over a decade with stints as a reporter and writer for a daily newspaper and a travel trade journal. Her writing has been published in anthologies, e-zines, and magazines.

Photo Credits

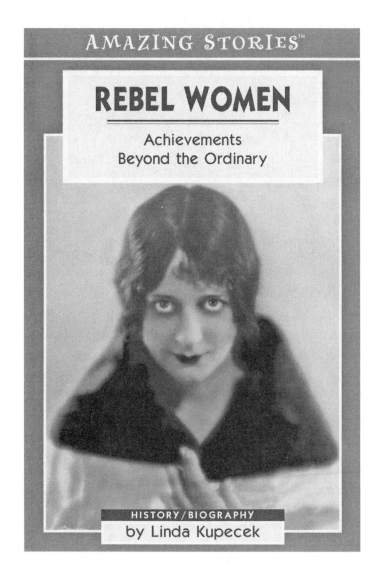

AMAZING STORIES™

REBEL WOMEN

Achievements
Beyond the Ordinary

HISTORY/BIOGRAPHY
by Linda Kupecek

REBEL WOMEN
Achievements
Beyond the Ordinary

"It seems to me there is always somebody to tell you [you] can't accomplish a thing, and to discourage you from even attempting it. If you are going to let other people decide what you are able to do, I don't think you will ever do much of anything."
Katherine Stinson

Many famous women of the west are celebrated elsewhere. In this book, we meet lesser known rebels, those who lived with passion, individuality, and courage. These are women who dared to follow their own path through life; women who dared to be different.

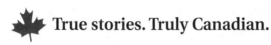 True stories. Truly Canadian.

ISBN 1-55153-991-8

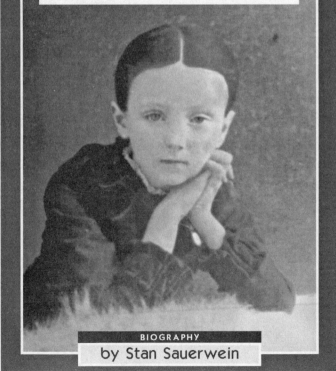

AMAZING STORIES™

LUCY MAUD MONTGOMERY

The Incredible Life of the
Creator of Anne of Green Gables

BIOGRAPHY

by Stan Sauerwein

LUCY MAUD MONTGOMERY

The Incredible Life of the Creator of Anne of Green Gables

"I set my teeth and said, 'I will succeed.' I believed in myself and struggled on alone.... I never told my ambitions and efforts and failures to any one. Down, deep down, under all discouragement and rebuff, I knew I would arrive someday."
L. M. Montgomery

L. M. Montgomery, the creator of Anne of Green Gables and author of more than 20 books, is a household name the world over. *Anne of Green Gables* has been translated into 40 different languages and immortalized on film. The spirited story of orphaned Anne was inspired by the natural beauty of Prince Edward Island.

 True stories. Truly Canadian.

ISBN 1-55153-775-3

TRUE CANADIAN
AMAZING STORIES™

KAREN KAIN

Canada's Prima Ballerina

BIOGRAPHY
by Melanie Jones

KAREN KAIN
Canada's Prima Ballerina

"Waiting backstage, Karen felt the jangle of her nerves grow silent as the sweet, soulful music began. She was no longer Karen Kain; she was Odette, the beautiful and tragic swan-maiden betrayed by her lover ..."

One of Canada's best-loved and most respected dancers of this century, Karen Kain's rise to ballet stardom is an inspirational story of dedication and passion. Now a national treasure, Karen Kain brought Canadian dance to the world's stage in the 1970s. This is a story of artistry and ambition — the joys and the sacrifices of a prima ballerina.

 True stories. Truly Canadian.

ISBN 1-55439-017-6

AMAZING STORIES™

THE LIFE OF A LOYALIST

A Tale of Survival in Old Nova Scotia

HISTORY

by Cathleen Fillmore

THE LIFE OF A LOYALIST
A Tale of Survival in Old Nova Scotia

"It was a dangerous time to be loyal to the Crown. The divisive war had pitted neighbour against neighbour and father against son."

The life of young Christiana Margaret Davis, a Loyalist born in upstate New York, was turned upside down by the American Revolution. A time of struggle and strife, she escaped with her family to Nova Scotia, finally landing on Brier Island in 1789. Her remarkable story sheds new light on the plight of Loyalists.

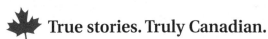 True stories. Truly Canadian.

ISBN 1-55153-944-6

ROBERTA BONDAR
The Exceptional Achievements of Canada's First Woman Astronaut

"The feeling in space flight is like hanging by your heels...with all the blood rushing to your head ... You feel as though you are at the top of a roller coaster when your stomach feels like it is going to lift off."
Dr. Roberta Bondar

From the age of eight, Roberta Bondar knew she wanted to be an astronaut. In January 1992 she made Canadian history when she became the first Canadian woman, and first neurologist, to go into space on board *Discovery*. The story of her journey to become a leading astronaut is a fascinating tale of dedication, commitment, and sheer guts.

 True stories. Truly Canadian.

ISBN 1-55153-799-0

AMAZING STORIES™

EMILY CARR

The Incredible Life and Adventures
of a West Coast Artist

HISTORY/BIOGRAPHY
by Cat Klerks

OTHER AMAZING STORIES

These titles are available wherever you buy books. If you have trouble finding the book you want, call the Altitude order desk at **1-800-957-6888**, e-mail your request to: **orderdesk@altitudepublishing.com** or visit our Web site **at www.amazingstories.ca**

New **AMAZING STORIES** titles are published every month.

EMILY CARR
The Incredible Life and Adventures of a West Coast Artist

"On a sketching trip with her friend Edythe Hembroff, Emily made the other woman swear not to peek while she hastily slipped into her nightie. This was odd considering how cheerfully Emily would defy social convention in many other ways. The woman who loved to shock others was quite easily shocked herself."

This is the story of a rebellious girl from BC who travelled the world in pursuit of her calling, only to find her true inspiration in the Canadian landscape she'd left behind. Despite numerous setbacks, she persevered. Today, Emily Carr is a Canadian icon. Her story is a testament to individuality and an inspiration to all.

 True stories. Truly Canadian.

ISBN 1-55153-996-9